CRUMBLING WALLS...

WHY PRISONS FAIL

CRUMBLING WALLS...

WHY PRISONS FAIL

By RUTH MORRIS

MOSAIC PRESS
Oakville - New York - London

CANADIAN CATALOGUING IN PUBLICATION DATA

Morris, Ruth, 1933–
  Crumbling walls-- : why prisons fail

ISBN 0–88962–410–0

1. Prisons. 2. Imprisonment. I. Title.

HV8665.M67 1988   365   C88–094814–0

Published by MOSAIC PRESS, P.O. Box 1032, Oakville, Ontario, L6J 5E9, Canada. Offices and warehouse at 1252 Speers Road, Units # 1&2, Oakville, Ontario, L6L 5N9, Canada.

Mosaic Press acknowledges the assistance of the Canada Council and the Ontario Arts Council in support of its publishing programme.

Copyright © Ruth Morris, 1989
Design by Rita Vogel
Cover Illusttration and design by Marion Black
Typeset Bambam Type & Graphics

Printed and bound in Canada.

ISBN 0–88962–410–0 PAPER

MOSAIC PRESS:
In Canada:
        MOSAIC PRESS, 1252 Speers Road, Units # 1&2, Oakville, Ontario L6J 5N9, Canada. P.O. Box 1032, Oakville, Ontario L6J 5E9

In the United States:
        Distributed by Kampmann & Co., 226 West 26th Street, New York, N.Y. 10001, USA, or Riverrun Press Inc., 1170 Broadway, Suite 807, New York, N.Y., 10001, U.S.A.

In the U.K.:
        John Calder (Publishers) Ltd., 18 Brewer Street, London, W1R 4A5, England.

TABLE OF CONTENTS

INTRODUCTION   7

The Wheels of Injustice   8

**PART I: THESE WALLS HAVE GOT TO COME DOWN:
THE CASE FOR PRISON ABOLITION**   10

   1. Prison Abolition: Lunacy or Practical Goal   11

   2. Prison Overcrowding   17

   3. Built-In Failure of Prisons:
      Frank Dunbaugh, Edgar Epp   24

   4. International Conference on Prison Abolition   29

   5. How to Get To Prison Abolition, Two Views:
      Virginia Mackle, Claire Culhane   35

**PART II: "INJUSTICE ANYWHERE CONCERNS
HUMANKIND EVERYWHERE"**   40

   1. Bail and Justice of the Peace:
      Pretrial Justice, An Early Struggle   40

   2. Stories of Individual Prisoners:
      Terry   80
      Steve   86

   3. Minorities In Our Justice System   96

   A. "One Indian's As Good As Another"   98

   B. Women In Prison   101

   C. The Noose, the Chain and the Needle
      (Capital Punishment)   107

**PART III: THE VISION BEYOND THE WALLS:
  TRUE ALTERNATIVES**   114

  1. Creative Alternative To Prisons:
      What Works Better?   115

  2. Toronto Bail Program   121

  3. Group Homes and The Struggle
      For Community Integration   137

  4. The Magic of Mediation:
      A First–Line Alternative   150

  5. What To Do With The
      Violent/Sexual Offenders   157

  6. The Spirit of True Alternatives   161

**PART IV: CONCLUSIONS: PRISON ABOLITION
  TODAY AND TOMORROW**   163

INTRODUCTION

This book consists largely of reprints, mostly of my own writings. It binds together most of my political writings on prison abolition: what it means, where it comes from, and whither it is leading us. Part I talks about prison abolition itself: the reasons we believe it is a necessity, and also some ideas about how to get abolition. Part II describes some of the bitter injustices of prison, while Part III asks what we would have instead of prisons. This has traditionally been called "alternatives," but because some alternatives are as obscene as prison, we have preferred to call this section: "The Vision Beyond The Walls."

It is our hope that these writings gathered in one volume can be a useful reader for University and High School classes and practitioners as well. It would be extremely refreshing if law students, from whom our future Judges and Crown Attorneys are drawn, had a little more idea of the real virtues of the prisons they send so many men and women to, with such infallible faith in the virtue of the remedy, despite the incredibly high failure rate. These doctors of the spirit blame the failure on the patients, and never seem to question the value of the prescribed medicine.

THE WHEELS OF INJUSTICE

By Art Solomon, Native Spiritual Leader

They say that
The wheels of justice,
They grind slowly.

Yes, we know.

But they grind
And they grind,
And they grind,
And they grind.

It seems like they grind
Forever.
And what they grind
Is Human Beings,
And how they grind.

They grind away
The Humanity
Of the victims
Who get caught
In its jaws.

Oh God, protect us
From a law abiding society.
Have pity on us,
Who are its victims.

Protect us, Oh God
From those who say
"We are Christians,"
Because we know
That if Christ
Walked visibly among them today,
They'd throw Him in jail tomorrow:
Oh God, protect us from law abiding citizens.

The wheels of injustice
    They grind forever.
But they have nothing at all to do with justice.
    Because
        The
            Name
                Of
                    The
                        Game
                            Is
                                Vengeance.

Oh God, protect us
    From
        The
            Game
                Called
                    Justice,
Where the rich get richer,
And the poor,
    They go to jail.

Yes, the wheels of injustice,
    They grind so slowly.
The Human Sacrifice is their meat.

    They grind the hopes and the dreams of some,
        While the parasites live in their homes of plush.
    Oh God, we are poor,
    Have pity on us,
    And protect us
        From the Law Abiding Citizens,
        Who turn the Wheels of Injustice.

PART I

THESE WALLS HAVE GOT
TO COME DOWN:

THE CASE FOR PRISON ABOLITION

Prison abolition is not a new idea. Eugene Debs wrote scathingly about the injustice of prison and its uselessness 65 years ago. A Washington Post Editorial in March of 1980 is titled: "Caging People Doesn't Work." The Kingston Whig-Standard in 1980 wrote a powerful editorial entitled: "Why Not Get Rid Of Canada's Penitentiaries?" This paper, in the heart of Canada's prison capital, Kingston, quoted a 1972 Wisconsin Council of Criminal Justice Report, which concluded that since prisons INCREASE crime, the Governor should do away with them.

Russell Baker has said wittily: "If we look at the American prison system the overwhelming logic of this becomes manifest: the American prison is primarily an educational institution. We send young men to prison, and they come out finished criminals, just as we send other young men to Yale and turn them into bankers.

"A constant supply of criminals turned out by our prisons contributes to economic health by maintaining full employment in the Police and Judicial industries, enriching lawyers and insurance companies, keeping social workers occupied, and supporting large government bureaucracies...

"A secondary purpose of prison is to provide storage space for poor people. In the criminal, legal and judicial classes, it is an established principle that the less wealth a felon has, the more time he must serve..."[1]

Why do so many people come to the same conclusion? In a nutshell, four groups of reasons can be crystallized in a single sentence: prisons are EXPENSIVE, UNJUST, IMMORAL FAILURES. Spreading these out more clearly, arguments against prisons fall into these four groups:

1)   EXPENSE: Prisons are more costly than any of their alternatives, and more costly than the public would pay for if it understood the price in dollars and cents alone.

10

2)   UNJUST: Prisons everywhere incarcerate the poor, minorities, and property offenders. Even if they were efficacious and efficient, a strong case could be made against them because they select the powerless to entrap.

3)   IMMORAL: As Canadian Quakers eloquently phrased it in a united statement in 1981, "We are increasingly clear that the imprisonment of human beings, like their enslavement, is inherently immoral, and is as destructive to the cagers as to the caged."

4)   FAILURES: Prisons are supposed to deter, protect, rehabilitate, and punish. In fact, they only do the last. They fail to deter others, to protect the public from crime or criminals, and they fail abysmally at rehabilitation.

The first article in this section, reprinted from *Canadian Dimension,* gives an overview of all four of these issues, while focussing more on that of injustice. Its basic point is that the strongest characteristic of prisoners is neither being bad nor sick, but being powerless. Therefore, neither punishment nor treatment can cure the problem. Only the just sharing of power can cure powerlessness.

1.
PRISON ABOLITION:
LUNACY OR PRACTICAL GOAL[2]

"Prisons represent our acceptance that some black, native, unemployed, and poor people are expendable..."
        (Walter Collins)

Before concluding that prison abolition is a form of lunacy peculiar to a few wild-eyed radicals, it is important to know who makes up the vast bulk of our prison populations:
1982 Ontario Ministry of Corrections statistics show that 37% of all admissions were for offences "against property," 12% for traffic offences, 18% for municipal violations, 14% for liquor and drug offences, and 7% for *offences against the person.* (See pie chart.)

Recent U.S. figures show that 42% of those who enter U.S. prisons are unemployed, and the average (median) income of those with any employment is $3200 per annum! The rate of incarceration for blacks is about 10 times that for whites, resulting in the logical assertion that U.S. prisons are a modern form of slavery. Rates of incarceration for Native people are similarly appallingly high in both our countries.

In short, the book title *The Rich Get Richer and The Poor Get Prison* is a very good summary of the function of prisons in our society. Our court system and our prisons are a socially acceptable tool for disposing of our surplus poor, unemployed, and minority groups. We reaffirm our social prejudices and inequities by stigmatizing these people as "criminals." Yet who causes the greater harm:

> An 18-year-old from a series of Children's Aid Homes who climaxes a "bad record" of running away from foster homes by committing a series of minor thefts;

> An employer who follows the good capitalist model by laying off 50 workers, creating waves of hardship in all 50 families, in order to increase his profit margin.

> A Native person who seeks to escape our society's lack of use for him through alcohol violations;

> A manufacturer who endangers his employees' and the public's health through pollution.

The 18-year-old and the Native person are criminals who will sooner or later serve time in our prisons, while the two capitalist employers are the respectable stuff of our society, praised for being good businessmen. The structural violence of our economic system, entrenched in the material rights of the powerful, is the foundation-stone of our courts and prisons.

The Dangerous Few

Having said that: "What about the dangerous few?" Or in current form, "What about the Clifford Olson's?" This is a legitimate concern and one which we prison abolitionists have to address. There are, both in and out of our prisons, a few persons who are truly violent and dangerous, who have been so damaged that they as well as society need to be protected from their most dangerous impulses. A number of points need to be understood about the dangerous few:

1. These people have already been punished by life. We do not need to wreak further vengeance on them. We do need protection from them.

2. Our present "justice system" is unlikely to sentence these few dangerous ones to consistently longer terms than many of the hapless multitude who make up most of our prison population. Instead, the prisons further damage and inflame the dangerous few, releasing walking time bombs into our midst.

3. Imprisonment itself is a major contributing factor to making some of the dangerous few dangerous. Olson himself was a 23-year graduate of our prison system before he committed his heinous murders.

4. Prison abolitionists for the most part favour humane, custodial, treatment-oriented solutions for the dangerous few. Abolitionists not only would not turn the Clifford Olsons out on the public; we are among the few actively seeking better solutions and ourselves working with the dangerous few.

5. By no means all of the dangerous few are in prisons. A world without prisons could deal more positively with prevention of root causes of all kinds of violence in our midst.

6. We must recognize that prisons are a costly fraud justified repeatedly to protect us from the dangerous few, when they neither protect us from them, nor even deal with them much more than many other social institutions. The excuse of the dangerous few is used to obscure the real function of prisons in reinforcing class and ethnic positions in a highly punitive and repressive way. It is comparable to the "Communist" red herring in diverting attention from the real issues, and from seeing the true picture of our "justice system."

13

Costs and Results: Prisons As An Investment

Another way of looking at the value of prisons is to consider their costs, and the return we get for this investment. The cost of keeping a person in a prison cell is higher than the best university education, and higher than all but the most exclusive hotels. Estimates vary from $56 a day in British Columbia to $87 per day in the NW Territories (current Ministry Figures). Canny prisoners have suggested that if they were given a reasonable portion of this money and told to go and sin no more, they could make a much more positive contribution to the community than by sitting in a prison cell.

Admissions to Ontario Prisons – 1982

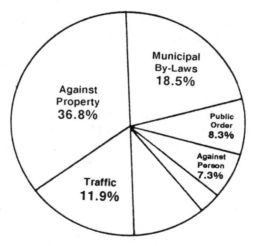

One has to add to this the cost of building new cells. Current estimates are about $100,000 – $200,000 per cell to construct a new cage for a fellow human being. In contrast to this, the most costly community alternatives, halfway houses, are about $30 per day, roughly half what it costs to keep a man or woman in prison, and there are further savings from such housing, for those living there can work and support their families, thus reducing welfare costs, and preparing themselves for reintegration into the community.

Most other community alternatives are much cheaper. The Toronto Bail Program provided pre-trial supervised release for those who could not afford bail, for just $2.40 per day per person! The cost of locking up its 500 clients for 2 weeks would have equalled the entire yearly budget of the agency.

Does this costly investment in prisons yield results? Recidivism figures vary depending on what is measured: committing the same offence or any offence, within a year, 2 years, 5 years. Using two years as a base, our most recent federal rates are 41%, but the younger the offenders, the more likely prisons are to give negative results. Thus 16-year-olds in Ontario with a prior history of legal problems have an 82% probability of reoffending within 2 years of release.

Although one can dicker over the extent of failure, no recidivism rates suggest that prisons meet minimum success standards. One educator commented after listening to prison recidivism rates: "We should study them – if we could get a return rate like that we'd really have learned something!"

Our attitude about what to do with offenders has moved from 19th century efforts to punish and terrify them into submission because they are bad, to 20th century values for rehabilitating them because they are sick. If the overwhelming characteristic of offenders is that they are powerless, then neither approach can work. You can't solve powerlessness by frightening or treating it, but only by being willing to share your power with it.

Reform: Has It Failed Or Never Been Tried?

Jessica Mitford in her book *Kind and Usual Punishment* has a chapter called "101 Years of Prison Reform," in which she details the many efforts to create reform in a prison atmosphere, and the failure of all. It is logically impossible to prove that reform could never work in some utopian institutional setting. But what we can say is that 100 years of efforts at prison reform have been virtually fruitless, even though in some cases like California, efforts have been extensive and apparently sincere.

Since criminality represents a temporary "bad fit" between some members of society and others, taking those judged unfit out of the community and making them adjust to an institutional atmosphere totally different from the community seems unlikely to resolve the bad fit. Logically, those well adjusted to institutional living are bound to be badly adjusted to community living.

Even if it were theoretically possible, our apparently unresolvable ambivalence between punishment and rehabilitation makes rehabilitation an unattainable goal.

It is powerless people who are imprisoned everywhere. You don't cure powerlessness by punishment or therapy. It can only be

cured by sharing power and resources in the wider society. Therefore, the whole philosophy of rehabilitation is based on a fundamental misunderstanding of our prisons and their functions.

The Movement for Prison Abolition:

It was out of this awareness, reinforced daily by the misery I
saw in courts and prisons, that the vision of an International
Conference on Prison Abolition was conceived. Our Quaker Committee on Jails and Justice provided the impetus that made it
happen. In May 1983, 400 persons from Europe, Australia, and North
America gathered in Toronto to address three major questions:

Why Do We Have Prisons?
How Do We Get to Abolition From Here?
What do we do with the tough cases; are there true alterna-
tives to prison?

Canadian Quakers had already made their position clear when
they adopted a ringing statement of faith in prison abolition, which
read in part:

*"Today Friends are becoming aware that prisons
are a destructive and expensive failure as a response to
crime. We are therefore turnng from   efforts to reform
prisons to efforts to replace them with non-punitive, lifeaf-
firming and reconciling responses. The prison system is
both a cause and a result of violence and social injustice.
Throughout history, the majority of prisoners have been the
powerless and the oppressed. We are increasingly clear
that the imprisonment of human beings, like their enslavement, is inherently immoral, and is as destructive to the
cagers as to the caged..."*

The response to the Toronto Abolition Conference was
impressive. A Steering Committee was established which planned
a Second International Conference in Amsterdam. A Newsmagazine was established, three issues of which have been distributed.
Repeatedly at Conferences I go to, I hear people talking about the
impact of the Toronto Conference, the prison abolition movement,
and the miracle that in times like this, such a birth could occur.

Conclusion

Today we are living in a strange political climate. Massive unemployment is accepted. Rightwing leaders and views predominate in may areas. Yet the peace movement and the women's movement manage to move forward with widespread support for many of their issues. Despite widespread support for true peace initiatives and against sexism in our society, we continue to elect governments whose actions conflict with these goals.

Perhaps one way to break through this strange deadlock is to recognize the interrelatedness of the many faces of justice. The Mennonites have a poster of a foot-shackled dove, and the words: "Crime is a Peace Issue." We cannot have peace without justice. Those who want peace will have to recognize that peace is not found in expecting the powerless and jobless and minorities to accept police violence, court stigmatization, and imprisonment as their lot. Sexism is intimately tied to all the other forms of discrimination woven into our criminal justice system. An end to prisons, and the building of a caring community which responds creatively to our differences, is the foundation of a world free from sexism and other discrimination, where peace is an inevitable outgrowth of our whole way of life.

2.
PRISON OVERCROWDING

The issue of prison overcrowding is closely related to that of prison abolition. The same factors that cause us to go on using an archaic and punitive prison system cause us to overuse it and overcrowd it. But the issue of what to do about prison overcrowding gives the abolitionist a dilemma: We don't want to join the doubly vengeful people who rejoice not only at caging their fellow humans, but rejoice even more if overcrowding makes the conditions of caging still more gross. Yet on the other hand, as abolitionists, we can hardly support prison building, particularly since the more prisons are built, the more the courts fill them. These issues are fully explored in the following article.[3]

* * * * *

I will never forget sitting in Supreme Court in Ontario, and hearing a Judge deny bail to a 19-year-old black single mother because she was "A danger to society to reoffend." She had initially been charged with a modest bounced cheque, and released to await trial on this charge. She then tried to do the proper thing and support her child by getting a cleaning job in a middle class home. Her employer missed some jewelry on her very first day, and charged her. Although the black mother denied taking it, and a search of her person and her home revealed nothing, she was arrested and denied bail. The denial was upheld in the hearing I witnessed, although she had no criminal record, denied guilt on both charges, and was looking after another child as well as her own. Consequently, two children suffered severe trauma of dislocation, and the woman faced months of incarceration before she could get a trial on either charge.

Uncommon? A bit more spectacular than most, but go and visit your local bail courts and see what you observe. Overuse of pretrial incarceration for cases where there is virtually no serious social danger is a major cause of jail overcrowding, and has very destructive effects on many lives.

Graham Stewart of Ontario John Howard Society amused a large conference on prison overcrowding with this analogy: "If I have an overflowing bathtub, there are three things I can do. I can pull out the plug, turn down the tap, or build an extra wing on my bathtub. If I try the last approach, chances are that long before I get it built, I'm going to need another wing, until pretty soon my whole house is dominated by a grandiose bathtub, and it's STILL overflowing."

Graham's story was funny because the overflowing bathtub owner's expansion mania was a perfect description of the North American correctional systems' solution to prison overcrowding; and their solution no more solves prison overcrowding than the frantic effort to build larger and larger bathtubs solves an overflowing bathtub. Why don't we try turning down the tap (slowing intake) or pulling out the plug (speeding release)?

For one of the inexorable rules people in the system know, but try to ignore, is: "As fast as Corrections can build them, the Courts will fill them." Indeed there is much empirical evidence that where a new jail or prison is opened, sentencing rates for minor offenders go up, and community alternatives are less effectively used, despite their greater success rates and much lower cost.

CRUMBLING WALLS: WHY PRISONS FAIL

Overcrowding Dilemma

Prison overcrowding poses a dilemma. Seeing double-bunking or even triple-bunking in cells built for one, the humanitarian in us cries out for more space for these human beings. This temptation is increased by many factors. Professor Des Ellis of York University summed up much literature on the connection between overcrowding and prison violence. Overcrowding is most likely to cause violence when the rate of transiency is high, the institution large, and the inmate population young. All these factors exist in many of our prisons today. In fact, the classification system in all penal systems increases transiency deliberately: people are moved up or down the maximum/minimum security ladder depending on how compliant the prison authorities believe them to be.

Opposition to new prison building seems to play into the hands of vindictive persons who want prisoners to suffer overcrowding and all its indignities as an added punishment to their trial, condemnation, and deprivation of liberty. The fact that prisons are overwhelmingly populated by the poor seems another powerful reason to avoid ghetto-like prison overcrowding.

Yet on the other hand, the more cells are built, the more will be filled. Moreover, rates of increase in incarceration are too high for prison building to keep up with them, as a sole solution. Canada and the U.S. already have among the highest rates of incarceration in the western world. Why do we need more cells? Canada incarcerates 109 persons per 100,000 and the U.S. rate is even higher. This contrasts with 26 per 100,000 in Holland, and similarly low rates in a number of Scandinavian countries![4]

North Americans are not four times as much in need of caging as Scandinavians. There is no reason for more cells to cage people. What we need is the will to use the many alternatives already available. They are cheaper and more effective for the vast majority of offenders, who are nonviolent property offenders. For this reason, many progressive Americans concerned about prison issues are actively promoting a "Moratorium on Prison Construction."

Yet their efforts meet with mixed success. Ironically, they are opposed by goodhearted people who believe humane prisons can reform. Moratorium advocates also have strange allies: those who think jampacked overcrowding is good enough for society's castoffs, and those who oppose any major public spending. The Moratorium movement is caught in a dilemma which contributes to the ambivalence whose end result is extreme prison over-crowding.

Easy Alternatives

But there are remedies readily available, if we have the will to use them. Recently I attended a health conference, and saw again in that field the same tragic social reaction. Where there are both institutional and community solutions to a problem, when budgets are tight, community programs are cut, and institutional beds and funds protected. Without wishing to see hospitals and their patients suffer, the irony of this is apparent – we always cut the moneysaving alternative in order to save money.

In prisons, this choice is even more starkly stupid. All the speakers at the recent Toronto Conference on Overcrowding pointed out that imprisonment for debt did not die with Dickens' novels: 37% of provincial sentences in Ontario in 1982-1983 were for fine default. Sean McConnville, a British criminologist, said this is the largest proportion he has seen in his studies in a number of countries. What a distinction for Ontario and for Canada!

Fine option programs exist in a number of jurisdictions. They enable the poor who can't afford to pay fines to work out the option, instead of going to jail. "$50 or 5 days," is no choice at all if you don't have $50. Yet, owing to the resistance of Roy McMurtry, and Ontario's Tory Government, efforts by a few enlightened corrections officials to establish fine option programs have made almost no headway. We are still running debtors' prisons on a large scale.

Another important option is pretrial release or bail programs. Setting of a money bail as a term of release is fine if you have a relative or friend with loyalty and means; for the poor, it means sitting in jail, sometimes for months, while you wait for trial. Bail programs provide professional supervised release for those who lack friends with means. Yet despite burgeoning pretrial populations, Ontario actually moved to cut its bail programs in 1983, and only kept them grudgingly, after heavy lobbying and strong editorial protest by both major Toronto papers.

About half of Canada's provinces lack bail programs in any form. It is surely a supreme irony that more people serve more time before trial than after conviction. As Alice in Wonderland said, "First we punish them, then we try them."

A more effective use of parole, and a more reasonable sentencing system could also turn down the tap and pull out the plug on prison overcrowding. "Capping" legislation in some American states has been effective. It legally requires prisons to release those nearest the end of their sentence, or classified least serious (depending on the law's wording), when crowding reaches certain limits. The illogically of sentence inequities is illustrated by the great differences in average provincial sentences: from 11 days in P.E.I. to 68 days in Manitoba.

Graham Stewart (Ontario John Howard Society) pointed out also that 500 people a year go to jail because of ADMINISTRATIVE VIOLATIONS OF PAROLE: acts not in violation of any law except some condition of their parole. He also noted that there has been a 31% increase in mean sentences in the last 10 years. In the same way that Manitoba offenders are no more vicious than those in P.E.I., today's offenders are no worse than those of 10 years ago: the variable is our will to cage people.

Discrimination Against the Poor

Excessive use of prisons and long sentences reflect our abuse of the poor. Few have said it more succinctly or aptly than our Ontario Liberal Justice Critic, Bob McKessock in a stunning report written in October of 1984. In it he cites this statement:

"Let's suppose I became philosopher-king and I could make any changes I wanted. Suppose I decided that minor social control offences, and crimes without victims were to be eliminated from the criminal code. Also, suppose minor property offenders were to be dealt with in the community rather than in jails. At the same time, suppose that I made tax evasion, knowingly polluting the environment, false advertising, fraudulent bankruptcy, and pricefixing, crimes which carried automatic jail terms. Now let's introduce the proverbial 'Man from Mars' who always gets into stories like this one. He arrives, and I take him on a tour of the Provincial Jail near Winnipeg. What would he say?...'You sure have a problem with your middle-class white people, don't you'?"
— Roland Penner, Attorney, Law Professor,
Former Chair of Legal Aid, Manitoba

McKessock himself continues: "Regardless of the bureau-cratic label you use to define poverty – Statistics Canada Poverty line, receiving general Welfare Assistance or Unemployment Insurance – the provincial jails are filled with impoverished inmates. This does not mean only the poor commit crimes. It does mean that in general, only the poor go to jail. It is not of course that they do not have options. 'The law in all its majesty forbids the rich as well as the poor to sleep under bridges on rainy nights, to beg in the streets, and to steal bread.' – Anatole France..."

Facts Of Overcrowding

Despite all the evidence of the destructive effects of institu-tionalization, of the justice system's discrimination against the poor, of the trivial nature of most offences for which people are serving time, and of the complete unfairness of pretrial incarcera-tion before conviction, there is a gross increase in prison use in both the U.S. and Canada. Bureau of Justice Statistics in the U.S. indicate a 47% increase in the pretrial, unconvicted population of U.S. jails from 1978 to 1983.[1] Sean McConnville reported that from 1973 to 1983 the prison population of the U.S. doubled! Canada's rate of increase is only slightly less alarming: our prison population doubled from 1950 to 1982.

Lest we take premature comfort in our modified infamy, we must add that McConnville, who has visited prisons in many countries, reported:

"CONDITIONS IN THE DON JAIL AND TORONTO WEST DETENTION CENTRE (two of the three Toronto Jails) RANK WITH THE WORST I HAVE SEEN IN ALMOST 20 YEARS OF VISITING OVERCROWDED INSTITUTIONS."

He described holding cells where people were almost shoul-der to shoulder, "Like being trapped in an elevator," and in sum called the conditions "A disgrace to this City and Province." He added that the smells of overcrowding permeated his clothes so heavily, he had to send them to the cleaners after the visits.

McKessock's conclusion is similarly strong and clear. Until 1981, during the years Glen Thomson was Deputy Minister of Corrections in Ontario, that Ministry had led out in creating and using effective new alternatives to prison. McKessock comments on the regression: "Many of the issues discussed in this report have burdened the corrections system in Ontario for decades: over-crowding, warehousing, rehabilitation. At one time, the Ministry of Correctional Services was regarded as a dynamic actor in the field of corrections and alternatives. NO LONGER."

McKessock's powerful final words are: "Overcrowding of detention and correctional institutions is the most persistent problem which haunts the Ministry of Corrections. Sadly, the Ministry has committed itself to the least creative and most expen-sive 'solution': expanding existing institutions and building more jails."[5]

Help From An Unexpected Quarter

One of the few effective steps against prison overcrowding has been the overcrowding suits brought by prisoners in a number of U.S. states. Some dramatic improvements have resulted from these suits - improvements which have not been realized by patient discussions with authorities.

Yet most social agencies which make their living from "helping prisoners" are funded by government, and are reluctant to raise issues and press for capping legislation and other strong solutions. When the Ontario Council for Community Alternatives to Prisons considered joining such a suit, several member agencies - includ-ing the Salvation Army and John Howard Toronto - withdrew, in fear of losing their funding, and in horror of a "confrontational approach." Yet the Ontario Ministry of Correctional Services had dragged its feet in responding to every effort toward dialogue for two years, during which the coalition made repeated offers to work cooperatively and supportively toward mutual solutions.

But amazingly, one group cared enough to initiate action: the Ontario Guards Union, a branch of the Ontario Public Service Employees Union! Unable legally to act officially as a union to sponsor a suit on overcrowding, a number of guards acting individually initiated a suit on behalf of the prisoners, against the overcrowding in the Ontario prisons and jails! This absolutely unprecedented event created some positive response by prisoners.

The Ontario guards don't just talk about professional standards. Unlike many of the social agencies and liberal citizens' groups, they have put their money quite literally where their mouths are. They are to be warmly congratulated, and it is hoped their example will inspire other groups, guards and reform groups alike, to consider similar action.

We do indeed live in an Alice in Wonderland time when we imprison more and more of the poor, and when helping agencies are afraid to help. But there will be more than a little compensation for all this if in Ontario, guards succeed in liberating prisoners from unjust overcrowding!

3.
BUILT-IN FAILURE OF PRISONS:
Perspectives by
FRANK DUNBAUGH and EDGAR EPP

For two years we ran a little newsmagazine called *The International Newsmagazine on Prison Abolition.* In it we published a number of articles on issues which the First Conference had made us aware of. The present section reprints two, both of which have a common theme. They demonstrate, from their own view, why prisons are bound to fail, by their very nature.

Frank Dunbaugh approaches the question as a lawyer and political activist. First he points out the systematic racism of the justice system in Maryland (and indeed everywhere else). Then he goes on to make the case powerfully that rehabilitation and prisons are inherently incompatible. He further links crime to many social ills, and points out we need to address these ills - unemployment, poverty, lack of housing - if we are to reduce crime.

Edgar Epp follows a similar theme, but unlike Mr. Dunbaugh, Edgar Epp has been a prison administrator, and a Deputy Minister of Corrections. His insider's knowledge of prison culture brings out again that it is in the VERY NATURE OF PRISONS that they destroy people further, and suck them into a vicious cycle.

Taken together, the two have a common, clear message: It is not just accidental that prisons breed recidivism; prisons are built-in, powerful, destructive systems which cling to and destroy those who fall into them. There is no change which can change this, for it is the very essence of prisons to destroy human beings.

FRANK DUNBAUGH'S TESTIMONY
TO MARYLAND TASKFORCE
JUNE 23, 1983

Two obvious truths influence my views on prisons:

FIRST – The practice of caging people is so degrading that its modern use can only be viewed as a continuation of the practice of slavery.

SECOND – America's prison system is the bucket into which falls the waste residue of our 350 year history of black slavery and racial discrimination.

There is no question that our shameful history of racial discrimination in education, jobs and housing has contributed significantly to the occurrence of those types of crimes for which we choose to cage people. The natural and inevitable consequences of our national tolerance for racial injustice and neglect are that black people have become the target of our criminal laws and of the various enforcement agencies, and, as a result, black people are put in cages in immensely disproportionate numbers.

Thus to fully appreciate what this Taskforce is dealing with, we must start by openly acknowledging that the State of Maryland engages in the practice of human enslavement, and that nearly all (about 4 out of 5) of its 11,000 slaves are black.

The Scope Of The Task

It would be a shame if this Taskforce were to limit its inquiry to the delivery of "rehabilitation and counselling programs" to persons confined in Maryland's prisons. In his letter, the Governor states his commitment to providing to prisoners an exposure "to a life style alternative other than crime." Is any other lifestyle possible in a prison?

Offenders on probation or parole can strengthen ties to their parents, loved ones, and children – ties which can improve their self image and sense of community values. Imprisonment destroys these ties. Being home allows an offender to be employed, to earn a living and to learn to take responsibility for oneself and one's family. Imprisonment relieves the offender of all responsibility.

Attorney General Levi once remarked that one of the most difficult problems is to reintegrate prisoners into free society. If the problem of reintegration is so difficult, one must wonder why we remove anyone from free society in the first place. Very few offenders need confinement. Those who do also need highly individualized attention in a calm, non-oppressive setting. No one should be caged.

To focus the State's resources on the imprisoned offender is, at best, a mistake. The so-called criminal justice system is like quicksand. Some people are in up to their ankles and getting in deeper. Others are up to their waists. The offenders who have reached the prisons are in quicksand up to their necks. Anyone up to his neck in quicksand cannot be expected to think of anything except getting out. Getting out is survival, and that is the first and last thing on every prisoner's mind. It is unrealistic to expect a drowning person to pay any attention to making plans for reform until after their escape from death.

Prisons teach disrespect for human life – a lesson which is antagonistic to any concept of rehabilitation which I can imagine. Besides, behaviour patterns which are appropriate in free society are dangerous in a prison, so attempting to teach such behaviour is fruitless.

Accordingly, if the State of Maryland is committed to helping offenders get their lives in order, the major effort should be made with probationers – offenders who live at home and function in the community, places where their lessons can be put in practice. But if we choose to help probationers develop their skills, we must relieve the probation agents of their police functions.

The Larger Picture

If the goal of rehabilitation is to teach offenders to live success-fully and lawfully in a free society, then shouldn't this Taskforce take into account the political and economic factors which prevent people from doing that? Zoning and public housing policies which force people to live in crowded conditions breed violence. Mone-tary and budgetary policies which ensure unemployment breed theft. Imprisonment fosters crime. Without an affirmative plan to alleviate these kinds of conditions, no amount of programming in the prisons will have a significant impact.

What kind of cruelty leads us to train a prisoner for a job that does not exist and then hold up his parole because he has no employment? And if we can train prisoners for meaningful employment, what sense does it make to require him to commit an offence to become eligible for this training?

Moreover, while there surely are prisoners who need training and counselling, there are many who are in prison because they exhibited the same characteristics we associate with success – goal setting, assertiveness, confidence, willingness to take risks. These are people who saw what they wanted and set out with determination to get it. So long as the business world is closed to them, criminal activity may be the only opportunity available for them to exercise their skills and sense of adventure. They are trying to live up to their potential in the only way they know how, which is very normal behaviour.

We live by materialistic, macho, competitive values that en- sure there will be winners and losers. If rehabilitative programs are successful in making "winners" out of the "losers" who are in our prisons today, what will we have gained. Won't they go out and make "losers" of someone else? No one can win without someone else losing.

It's as if we were all in a greased pit of snakes. None of us will get out until we abandon fighting one another and realize that we must work together for the survival of all.

THE DYNAMICS OF PRISONS
Extracts From Conference Address by EDGAR EPP

The task that I have taken on is to look at the prison system. That system represents only 1.3% of all crime. Prisons represent that end of the system where we put the most readily detected, the most readily prosecuted, and the most readily forgotten about.

We have prisons because we have come to believe in them, even though they do represent only 1.3% of total crime, and even though some 98% of those who go in come back into the community. We don't think about the fact that for every 100 prisoners who went in the front door today, 98 were released out the back door. It's really only a revolving door. Prisons represent a temporary warehouse where goods will eventually come out. But what if those goods are then more spoiled?

There is no good research showing the extent to which the crime problem has been caused by the system itself. That's the point which I wish to address this evening. I want to address the problem created by the prison itself.

Every new admission poses a threat to the other prisoners. The other prisoners have a vested interest in knowing who this person is. Is he "planted" here? Is he someone whom we can trust, who will not give away our secrets? You know, such things as: Who is planning to go over the wall?...Who is hiding a knife in his cell?...Where is the hootch stashed?...Which staff person will "kite" things in and out?...Where is the pipeline for the drugs?

As the new prisoner might give away that information, it is imperative that he be brought into line as quickly as possible. It will happen in different ways, but it might happen something like this: At the cafeteria, the inmate will be jostled. Or, as they are lining up for their work assignments, there will be some shoving and pushing. The new prisoner will be told to "watch it!" Something will happen that will throw fear into the new prisoner, who may already be full of fear.

Shortly afterward, some other prisoner will say something like, "I heard you had a little rumble the other day." ... or ... "You know, this is a pretty rough place."

By then, there will already be a kind of dossier on the new prisoner. Key prisoners in the institution will know who this person is, who his friends are inside and outside, what he is in for, whether it is the kind of crime that can be respected.

At that point a 'bargain' may be struck. Every large prison has a protection racket among the prisoners themselves. New admissions will fit into that racket. If they are not part of those who protect, they will be part of those who pay for protection.

Payments may be cigarettes or canteen goodies, but commonly it will be sexual favours. If a prisoner wants to stay alive and healthy in the institution, he will pay for protection as required. There are many people who have wondered why a prisoner tried to escape just two days before he was to be paroled. The reason may be: he didn't pay for his protection or for his gambling debt. He was told, "You better pay before they spring you, or they will carry you out." When faced with that kind of alternative, one very often gambles on being able to get away undetected, perhaps even be shot at by a guard who might miss, rather than staying inside where they won't miss!

Every prisoner also knows that in order not to be "fingered" he has to appear free of all suspicion. Even spending too much time in the chaplain's office can put one under suspicion. Being too friendly with one of the corrections officers or counsellors is cause for suspicion.

A prisoner who wants to get through prison alive and healthy does not dare become rehabilitated. There is no way that a prison can be rehabilitative, because these dynamics are at work. It is into this situation that we are condemning men and women.

The first prison sentences two hundred years ago were at maximum six months. It didn't work, so we doubled it and tripled it, until what used to be six months can now be twenty-five years! It still doesn't work. Yet, instead of checking our diagnosis, we have simply increased the dosage. I am suggesting that it CAN'T work.

It can't work because the dynamics of the system itself are basically counter-productive. There is no alternative but to get rid of the system, and to devise a more realistic approach that, at least, does not work against itself.

4.
INTERNATIONAL CONFERENCE ON PRISON ABOLITION

In 1982 I dreamed an incredible dream, of our little Quaker Committee on Jails and Justice sparking the First International Conference on Prison Abolition. Bob Melcombe, Jake Friesen, Ronny Yaron, Jonathan Rudin, Barbara Yip, and a few others made it their dream, and we gave a year of our lives to making it reality. It was an absurd undertaking. I used to say it was an idea whose time had come because we were determined to MAKE it come. I also said that we brought it off because we were too dumb to know that with the resources we had, it was impossible, so we went ahead and did it anyway. With no government funding, with about six totally committed people, we planned and executed a major International Conference with 400 registrants and representatives from over a dozen countries, at a time when things were moving backward, not forward!

So one night in May of 1983, I found myself on the stage, opening a First International Conference, with this introduction:

OPENING INTRODUCTION TO 1983 TORONTO CONFERENCE ON PRISON ABOLITION

A few years ago I was asked to give the presentation at the annual gathering of Quakers across Canada on why we Quakers in Canada should take a position endorsing prison abolition. Contrary to the impression you might have if I'm the only Quaker you've met, not all Quakers are ardent prison abolitionists, anymore than all Catholics, Anglicans, Jews, or humanists are. So it was a formidable prospect.

What came to me then was a vision based on an old story of a little child who said: "Someday they're going to call a war, and nobody will come." When we ask the world to look toward prison abolition, all we are really saying is this:

> "Someday they're going to build a prison,
> And there won't be anybody to put in it.
> There won't be anybody because you and I
> Will have opened our hearts, our homes, and our
> communities,
> And found better ways of dealing with our social
> differences
> Than by locking and caging our fellow human beings."

That's all prison abolition is about, and when you look at it that way, it's not so frightening or overwhelming. It is a vision of the caring community, the community that in our hearts we would all like to live in. It is gaining security not by locking our doors against the bad people out there, or locking those bad people up in prisons; but by making the whole community a safe, caring, positive place for everyone.

In trying to develop a conference to deal with prison abolition, I saw at the outset that we needed three themes, and you will find these themes running right through the conference. We could of course spend the whole conference bemoaning the evils of prisons, and not be a step nearer the prisonless society. It is far easier to criticize than to create, but this is a conference to create. To do that, we have to answer three questions:

1) Why do we have prisons?
2) How can we begin to move away from them?
3) What do we want in place of them?

A.   ANALYZING THE SYSTEM. Nothing exists without a reason. The justice system is not wholly evil, nor is it uncaused. It represents our efforts at this point to deal with some very real problems. If we are to develop better ways of dealing with those problems, we have to understand the existing system, what functions it serves, and therefore what needs we have to meet in order to replace it.

B.   HOW TO GET TO ABOLITION FROM HERE. Given the real world, and the real people and problems in it, what can we do NOW that will be a practical and positive step toward a world without prisons, not just another band-aid helping the imprisoning society continue to separate and categorize us.

C.   WHAT TO DO WITH THE TOUGH CASES: TRUE ALTERNATIVES TO PRISON. In some ways this is the most critical area of all. Originally we were going to have workshops to deal with each of the groups we felt hardest to fit into existing community solutions: the few truly dangerous ones, the acting out mentally ill, the chronically institutionalized, and the extremely rebellious adolescent. But we decided the right kinds of solutions applied to more than one of these groups, so instead we grouped workshops by kinds of approaches in the prisonless society to all these difficult groups. These are called 'True Alternatives to Prison' because they are fundamentally different from present alternatives in one vital respect: you don't have prison as a fallback.

Before I introduce our first speaker, I just want to say one more thing. When I presented prison abolition to that gathering of Canadian Friends, I had no serious expectation that they would unite that very week in support of prison abolition, but they did.

When I dreamed of this conference, I could not have envisioned standing here tonight with this wonderful audience of people from many countries, and an exciting three days of events before us, a historic step forward toward the prisonless society.

I have seen too many impossible miracles happen when you have the courage to follow your dreams to call anything impossible. But you can make the future we need impossible by remaining locked in the prison of your own lack of imagination.

Or you can move forward with us,

Dream the dream of a future without prisons,

And begin to work toward it right now.

*   *   *   *   *   *

The Conference was a monumental event. It bore bitter as well as sweet fruits. When we launched the newsmagazine from the Conference, I wrote the first editorial, commenting on both kinds of fruits:

INTERNATIONAL NEWSLETTER – PRISON ABOLITION

Making The Dream Reality

Only a little over a year ago, some of us came up with the dream of a Conference on Prison Abolition to be held in Toronto. All of you joined us in making that dream a reality, and in making that reality an achievement beyond our dreams. The inspiration of knowing so many of you, of hearing the steps you are taking and the hopes you have, more than fulfilled our vision for the First International Conference on Prison Abolition.

One conferee wrote us that people in her prison had greeted her return with these words: "Welcome back to reality." We have all had to return to our hard realities. Mine was as harsh as any, for I was in the process of being fired on issues of principle when the conference took place, and that process has now been completed. Knowing throughout the conference what was to come afterward, gave it a poignant special beauty for me.

But the conference and everything else I have experienced in life convince me again and again that our faith in prison abolition is as hard-rock reality as the rigid rules of courts, the harsh responses of system-hardened guards, or as those too, too solid prison bars.

It is the spiritual power of our absolute conviction that prison abolition must come that will continue to move us forward. A few years ago a member of our Friends Meeting spoke these words in our Meeting: "After being in the Don Jail Volunteer Program every week for over a year; after meeting the men there week after week, and sharing their lives, I have no final answers except for this certain knowledge: These walls have got to come down. I don't know how, or how soon, but I know with all that is in me, THESE WALLS HAVE GOT TO COME DOWN."

Brick by brick, as we build the International Movement for Prison Abolition, we are taking down those walls. Toronto gave birth to an infant movement, and now all over the world those of us linked together are nurturing its development. Through this news-letter and this movement, we look forward to building with you a world without prisons.

The Conference put in closer touch abolitionists from the U.S.A., Canada, Europe, and Australia, with a few from other parts of the world. The First Conference had these stated goals:

1)   To inspire those already committed to prison abolition, by gathering many of us together to strengthen our mutual dedication to a world without prisons.

2)   To exchange ideas and think creatively together about how to achieve prison abolition, and what conditions must go with it.

3)   To educate the general public on the failure of prisons, and the need for new thinking in this area.

4)   To address the questions of those who believe prisons have failed, but wonder about the meaning and practicality of abolishing them.

Looking back on it, we believe we made significant progress toward each of those goals, but with the First Conference, we reached more of the grassroots: workers in the field and exprison-ers. The Second Conference, in Amsterdam, was focussed a little more on academics, though it still included a mix, and a still wider variety of nations. In my closing editorial of the Newsmagazine, I talked about where the Amsterdam Conference was leading us:
"Amsterdam confirmed that we are on the track of something that must not, can not, and will not be stopped.
"Amsterdam also made clear that we are broadening our vision as we gain momentum even in these back-facing times, as to what needs to be abolished. The Toronto Conference laid the ground for seriously addressing, at a major International Confer-ence, the abolition of prisons.
"The Amsterdam Conference, perhaps because it was more academic, broadened the challenge: the focus of abolition included the whole judicial-court system."

In my own summary of the Second Conference, as part of the closing panel, I made two suggestions for us to think about in relation to the Third Abolition Conference:

1)   ABOLITION OF POLICE.
Our French panelist united with me in the suggestion that we look at the most universally violent "justice" institution of them all, and question why in every country I have examined, we foster an institution which promotes violence. The police sector appears to be the most violent, illegal, and inhumane aspect of a system already abysmally destructive. This awareness was stimulated by our visit to the Dutch prison, where a black prisoner told me of being held four days by the police in this humane country, and having to drink toilet water because he was offered no liquid.

2)   INTEGRATION OF PRACTITIONERS AND ACADEMICS.
The Toronto Conference was run by and for people immersed in work with prisoners, and by prisoners themselves. The Amsterdam Conference was centered on a campus, and included academics from many countries of Europe. There is no right or wrong in these two approaches, which along with the religious approach, weave together to form the cloth of abolition. But ideally, the Third Abolition Conference should weave all the threads closer together.

Academics have much valuable research, theory, and perspective on which to build abolition. Religious roots offer the vital spiritual basis for abolition. And those immersed in the system offer the day to day realities, to keep us all in touch with the real people and challenges we have to deal with to build abolition in this world and era. In the Third Conference, we need to bring all these together to build a basis for abolition so well founded, it will move forward through every possible obstacle.

5.
HOW TO GET TO PRISON ABOLITION: TWO VIEWS
By Virginia Mackie and Claire Culhane

But one of the most important obstacles to abolition is the self-perpetuation of the system itself. The Americans who pioneered years ago in writing *Instead of Prisons,* advocated getting to abolition through what they called the attrition model: take one group after another out till there is no one left. Virginia Mackie, at the Conference, described this model more fully:

ATTRITION MODEL FOR PRISON ABOLITION
Virginia Mackie: Address at ICOPA - May 1983 (Abridged)

The process of abolishing prisons is very complex. You cannot work only on a rational basis. You have to begin to get at people's fears and emotions. When you realize that it's a prison industrial complex in the same way that it's a military-industrial complex, then you realize you're up against powerful forces. So how do you begin?

I think most of us began over some recognition of injustice. For many of us, it was simply the inequities and the discrimination which leads to poor people and people of colour occupying our nations' jails and prisons. Some began over concern over victims. In any event, we began. We tend to use the management by objective model:

1) Focussing the problem;
2) Learning as much as we can about it;
3) Spelling out our strategies;
4) Getting together our allies.

In 1974-75 some of us, including Faye Honey Knopp, began spelling out the attrition model of prison abolition. When you use a word like abolition it tends to send shock waves through people. They think we're talking about demolition.

So we began to spell out "What could we do?" If we are going to be serious about abolition, we have to take a long view and we have to be clear about our vision. First of all, we need a *moratorium* on prison construction. You have to say STOP. No more! Stop expanding! Put a cap on the prison population.

Next step in the model is how can you *decarcerate?* How can you keep people out of prison? The greatest number of people experience jail at the pre-trial level. So that's where you can make the greatest difference.

Third, how can you *excarcerate,* i.e., get people out who are already in there? There are lots of good models. So you begin to realize the biggest problem is will. How do you influence public policy to effect moratoriums, decarceration, and excarceration?

In your introduction to this conference, you have indicated that for prison abolitionists, it is important to think not only about alternatives within the system, but alternatives to the criminal justice system. We have to put into place community based alternatives so that people never go into the criminal justice system, or if they do go in, to the least extent possible. This takes caring. It takes you and me opening up our hearts and putting into place the kinds of systems that are going to keep people from having to go into the criminal justice system. It takes alternatives to the adversarial system.

Finally we ask, what do we do about the dangerous few? Because some people are so damaged or violent, for their own safety or that of others they will have to be removed from society for some periods of time. The attrition model says that if this is necessary, it must be in humane environments, small residential communities, not cages, not huge institutions. This is the attrition model, always keeping the vision of abolition, but being able to take these steps.

There are three values underlying the abolition model:

ECONOMIC & SOCIAL JUSTICE: Recognizing the ties between imprisonment and the isms - racism, classism, sexism, patriarchalism, that leads to oppression.

CONCERN FOR ALL VICTIMS: Recognizing many of the people who go through our criminal justice system as victims of oppression themselves.

RECONCILIATION.

This brings us to another point of concern listed in the conference program: alternatives. What are the reconciling, restoring, redeeming, recreating ways in which we can deal with our social problems? We have a very fixed punitive mindset, and again that gets back to the fact that we're dealing not only with social problems but with values and emotions. Why do the wicked prosper? How do I make myself righteous without a scapegoat? How do we stop blaming?

The single most creative alternative to the criminal justice system and the adversarial process is preventive mediation and conciliation. So through the inter-religious Taskforce in the U.S.A. we are beginning to spell out an "interfaith conciliation initiative." We want to build on programs that have been around a long time, such as Victim Offender Reconciliation Programs. We want to make sure people in the religious community are aware of them so that they can begin to put them in place in every community across the country.

We're also talking about neighborhood justice models: community boards in San Francisco; Quaker groups in Philadelphia. In Rochester where we're working in a crime prevention project at a neighborhood level, we're hoping to make the community board mediation/conciliation method a prime resource. This model allows people to deal with more of their conflicts and disputes before they erupt into violence.

Another value of the conciliation method is that it gives people the sense that they can solve their own problems. It uses neighborhood people to do the mediating.

Finally, we're concerned about it as a vehicle for resolving community-wide social conflicts, the kind of problems you have in Wounded Knee or Kent State, or in a plant closing or an immigration border dispute.

Because I represent a religious perspective, I want to say a word about some of the work we're doing to try to find alternatives to punitiveness. One of the reasons I think this important is that the justification for punishment is very frequently associated with religious roots. How often have you heard the phrase, "an eye for an eye and a tooth for a tooth"? This is a misinterpretation of the old Judaic LexTalionis. So we must go back to our religious roots to ask, "How did we get here? What went wrong? How was Christianity in particular tied to political systems and power that led to the state controlled criminal justice system?"

So how do you go about working for prison abolition?

First, be very clear about your vision.

Secondly, develop your organizing skills, and look for your allies.

Thirdly, we need to develop a much greater critical consciousness. We need a better historical perspective. We need to look at ourselves.

We need to evaluate the values from which we operate, because the kind of world-view that supports prisons is a very consistent world-view. It grows out of the whole competitive ethic, the oppressive ethic, and probably the capitalistic economic ethic.

If we're going to change this society so that we can have the kind of framework in which we can convince people to work for abolition, we have to begin thinking about our own ethics and world views; our own sense of community and relationships, as well as our organizing skills.

* * * * *

However, Claire Culhane, leading Canadian abolitionist, offers another model for how to get prison abolition: civil disobedience. Although not totally opposed to the attrition model, Claire points out how often steps which seem to be taking one or another group out are diluted and diverted. She believes they must be combined with something strong enough to get the message across unequivocally. Claire concludes an editorial she did in our Newsmagazine:

"Two roads face us as we search for the most expedient solution to the present chaos in the prison system:

"Accept the trend towards control, which historically begins with the most vulnerable section of the population - in this instance, prisoners...

OR

"Dismantle the billion dollar prison industry with all its vested and political interests.

"The most effective contribution to the abolition of prisons would be to join forces with those fighting for universal abolition of poverty, abolition of war, and abolition of injustice."

Claire's voice is a fitting one with which to conclude this opening section on the basic case for prison abolition. The next section on injustices and the final section on true alternatives round out the case for why we need abolition, where we are going, and how to get there.

CRUMBLING WALLS: WHY PRISONS FAIL

NOTES

1.   Russell Baker, "Prison Term Ruled Out," *New York Times, August 31, 1974.*

2.   First printed in *Canadian Dimension*, Vol. 18, No. 4, 1984.

3.   Article on Prison Overcrowding printed in slightly altered form first in *Canadian Dimension*, Vol. 19, No. 4.

4.   Bastien, Lopanco & Starkman, 1984, John Howard Society, Ontario, 46 St. Clair East, Toronto, Ontario, "Prison Overcrowding Report."

5.   Quoted in Moratorium Working Papers #32, UUSC National Moratorium on Prison Construction, 1251 – 2nd Avenue, San Francisco, California, 94122, U.S.A., by Andy Hall.

6.   McKessock, Robert, MPP, *Behind Prison Walls: Justice For All.* Queens Park, Toronto, Ontario.

PART II

"INJUSTICE ANYWHERE CONCERNS HUMANKIND EVERYWHERE"

1.
BAIL AND JUSTICES OF THE PEACE: PRETRIAL JUSTICE, AN EARLY STRUGGLE

Logically, my first major battle in the justice system was with the bail system and Justices of the Peace. This came about because my first volunteer work was in the jails, which are overflowing with people waiting for trial, who have not yet been convicted. I soon found out that although Justices of the Peace are one of the oldest established groups of officials, they are largely selected from the ranks of court clerks who get promoted, and other political appointments; they have few specific qualifications for their work; they have appallingly unlimited power in some areas, with few clear public guidelines, and almost no direct appeal from some of their decisions on sureties. As a would-be surety for some of my prisoner-friends, I began to experience being treated as a nonperson by a number of JPs, and became increasingly agitated on the subject. I battled with it directly for about four years, until I ran into a series of dead ends on the issue, and my new position as Director of the Toronto Bail Program enabled me to do some things about unjust pretrial incarceration, while preventing me from continuing my assault on the particular injustices perpetrated by JPs.

The subject deserves a book in itself, and I have enough case material on it to write one, but I think a selection here will illustrate what an important issue of injustice is found in pretrial detention.

In November of 1978, after three years of frustration, I wrote a letter to a number of officials:

LETTER TO OFFICIALS ON JPs AND BAIL

For nearly three years I have been working as a volunteer in the justice system, visiting jails and prisons, court watching, and becoming involved in all aspects of the process.

I have a deep concern for the whole bail system, which seems to me one of the aspects of our justice system where justice is poorest and most inconsistent. Moreover, it seems very hard to come by reliable information about it. I have talked with numerous experienced and well qualified lawyers, with some legislators, and with the Crowns' Office, and am frequently told that I know as much about the bail and JP system as they do. What I would like to present are a number of problems with questions about them.

A. INCONSISTENCY OF JUSTICES OF THE PEACE AND THEIR APPARENT ABSOLUTE POWER

I am referring here principally to JPs involved in approving or rejecting sureties for bail, not to those with even greater authority who make judicial rulings in lower courts on whether a person merits bail at all, and for how much. I have watched many bail hearings conducted by JPs and have deep concerns about the quality of justice there too, but that is another subject. I know that some JPs conduct hearings and sign bails, but gather that some are only qualified for bail signing, and it is this latter area of bail signing I am speaking about now.

From my first contacts with the justice system, I began hearing regular complaints from prisoners and their families about repeated inconsistencies and arbitrary rejection of sureties by JPs. One of the very cruel things in the way it is usually handled is that a prisoner is usually brought down and told he is or may be getting bail, and then has the bitter disappointment of being told he is not, if the surety is rejected by the JP. This a form of mental torture which could easily be avoided by not bringing down or informing a prisoner of possible bail until a JP has decided whether the surety is acceptable. If the term mental torture seems strong to you, you should visit a person who has just been through the experience of being told he is getting out and then being sent back to the unit.

With regard to the acceptability of sureties, we hear of many cases where persons are rejected by a JP on no very specific grounds, and are often later accepted by another JP if they have the nerve, persistence, and knowledge to keep coming back. Needless to say, it is very unpleasant if they come back and encounter the original JP again. As one JP said to me last week, "I don't have to justify or explain my decision to you."

It is difficult to document clearly, but there is certainly a lot of evidence that JPs suffer from the same class bias as the rest of us, and reject many people because they look poor or unsavoury. Since most people in trouble with the law are poor, and their relatives and friends are poor, the prisoner and his surety start out with one strike against them.

These problems suggest the following questions:

1)   Are there any guidelines at all for JPs to use in determining who is and is not acceptable as a surety? What are they, if they exist, and under whose authority were they created and are they administered? How does one go about changing any that need modification?

2)   What checks and balances can be set up to provide counterweight to the potential abuse of the absolute power that seems given to JPs?

3)   Recognizing that some discretion inevitably must be given to JPs on who is an acceptable surety, should there not be a practical, known system of appeal to protect the individual from absolute power? What systems of appeal exist, how practical are they for the average individual, and how can they be made more widely known and usable?

4)   Could some system of recording JP interviews with sureties be used to insure accountability of JPs?

B.   QUALIFICATION AND TRAINING OF JPs

I am very interested to know what qualifications JPs have, and how they are selected; what training they undergo for their great responsibilities, and under whose authority they come. I can find little information on this, except that the Crown's Office believed that were under authority of the Head Judge, but also thought they might be partly responsible to the Crown directly. My questions then are:

1) What are the qualifications of a JP?

2)   Can the training process do more to limit class bias and make the JP aware that he is fundamentally a public servant? The attitude of some, fortunately by no means all JPs, that they owe neither courtesy nor accountability to any member of the public who comes to them, needs correction sorely.

3)   Can the authority in charge of JPs be made more clearly known, so that a line of accountability is established? In this way when problems arise, one would have some idea where to go, instead of being faced with battling a cloudy mist of cotton wool.

C.   HOW MANY PEOPLE CAN A SURETY HAVE ON BAIL

The immediate provocation for this letter is the continued aggravation of unclarity on this question. Occasionally JPs insist that a surety can only have one person on bail at a time, and on two occasions I have been turned down on this ground. Our ability to cover financially both existing bails and the proposed one was not at issue. These JPs have not cited any legal basis or rational reason for their position, and most JPs do not appear to think the issue relevant. Nonetheless, the unclarity means that most of us working in this field are constantly handicapped by the possible application of this absurd idea.

Given that caseloads for probation and parole are anywhere from 30 to 70 or more, there is something utterly preposterous in saying that a dedicated professional volunteer like myself cannot supervise adequately two persons at once on bail. Parents somehow manage to look after more than one child in many families. Thus I see no rational basis for an arbitrary limit of one.

Any concerned, informed volunteer in corrections encounters worthy cases from time to time of people awaiting trial who have bail but lack a local surety with property or funds sufficient to meet it. It is in every sense to the benefit of the total community and the taxpayer as well as the persons awaiting trial if such people can receive reliable supervision from volunteers such as myself, rather than remain in jail for the entire period till trial. By ANY standard of justice, punishment before trial should certainly be avoided whenever possible.

Moreover, even in the case of those eventually adjudged guilty, it is far more appropriate to encourage them in the waiting period to demonstrate responsible working and living patterns and support themselves and their families, rather than suffer the further debilitation and forced inactivity of our jails, while costing the taxpayer about $400 per week per inmate.

Recognizing all this, government officials have frequently given lip service to wanting to clear out of jails unnecessary cases, and keep inmate population to a minimum. One concrete way of doing this is by a more rational policy toward bail sureties, making clear that one person one bail is NOT acceptable. I know of at least two cases where persons have been on bail in long appeals for 2-3 years. Does this mean that the one or two persons involved as sureties in each of these cases can help supervise no one else for such major portions of their working lives? I would challenge anyone to examine the kind and depth of supervision I give to those I have on bail, and conclude whether or not the public is better off with these people taking steps toward more effective living rather than languishing in jail, growing in bitterness, and losing touch with all of life except newer and better approaches to crime.

In sum, I have just two questions about this matter:

1)   Is there any legal basis whatever for the one person - one bail concept?

2)   If so, how can we change it? Or if not, how can we make clear to JPs that it is not an acceptable standard?

I apologize for the length of this letter, but it is a matter I have lived and suffered with for several years now. There are many other vital aspects I have not even touched on, such as the pressure on innocent persons to plead guilty, when held in custody for long periods, unable to make bail. I would like some answers to the questions I have raised, and to see if we as concerned Canadians can act to improve the quality of Canadian justice in relation to bail.

*   *   *   *   *

These concerns arose out of several years of frustrations. Among the most heartbreaking of these were two cases where I was turned downed as a surety solely on the ground that I had one other person on bail at the time. This rule does not exist in writing, and as will be seen later in this section, was denied by the Attorney General's Office in a legislative hearing, but it exists in the minds of a random number of JPs, who apply it with tragic results. I had never heard of it till that day in 1977 which is described below.

FAMILIES, FRIENDS, AND BAIL – 1977

Because of our work in jails and justice programs, we are sometimes approached by friends of people needing bail to see if any of our group would be able to help out in a particular case. This happened recently in relation to Karen Ward, a young woman who needed two bail signatures with $8000 property each, plus a $500 cash deposit. Her boyfriend was prepared to be the one property surety, and the cash was available, but there was a need for a second surety.

After hearing full details of her case, and after discussing it with mutual friends of Karen's and ours, my husband and I agreed we would be the other surety. We met Karen's boyfriend and lawyer and together went to the Don Jail, where a visit with Karen for me had been arranged.

Karen was of course delighted that after some weeks in the Don, she was finally to be released on bail. She was very moved and very grateful and our visit was a beautiful occasion. I didn't even particularly mind that the JP was an hour later than he had said he would he.

This particular JP appeared hostile and obstructive from the beginning. I am certain I did not imagine this, because I find going bail for someone a very beautiful and moving experience, and my generally warm feelings extended to the JP as well as everyone else in the situation. He began by arguing that what was required was $1000 cash, not $500, because the $500 cash deposit was mentioned after the phrase about two sureties, so could have been meant as $500 from each. Without the lawyer present we would probably have been defeated for that day, since the banks were just closing and nothing but cash or certified cheques are acceptable. But since our lawyer had been in court when the paper was written, she eventually persuaded him that $500 was what was intended.

The JP then proceeded to cross-examine me in what I can only describe as a cold and somewhat hostile manner. Even so, I was not at all disturbed since my husband and I are so full of all the hallmarks of middle class respectability it never occurred to me he could find any ground to turn me down. Also, in spite of all our experience in the justice system, I still had difficulty conceiving why he should want to. What satisfaction could he get out of taking a woman on the threshold of hope and freedom, and finding some pretext for dealing her a crushing blow and sending her back into custody just when she knew she was to be freed?

We settled the question of a criminal record or charges for me, and whether my husband knew of my intentions to sign our property as bail. Then he began asking me if I had signed bail for someone else. I stated frankly that I had, that I was one of two signatures for a young man in Milton, and that his trial was in progress but not yet over. Abruptly, the JP stated, "Then I can't accept you as a surety."

Our lawyer pressed him repeatedly to explain his position for at least 15 minutes. He was not interested in the question of whether we had financial resources to cover both. He did not question my personal or moral capabilities. It was simply a hard and fast rule *with him* that no one person could possibly fill all the onerous tasks of a bail surety for two people at once.

He also stated that a bail surety has three obligations:

1) To see that the person bailed out behaves in a moral and responsible way and does not get into further trouble.

2) To see that the person bailed out carries out all incidental provisions of the bail provisions, such as reporting to police stations, refraining from certain contacts, etc.

3) To see that the person bailed out gets to court on the days required.

Although this JP tried to insist all three were legal obligations, a thing which frightens many – who can guarantee another human being will behave perfectly? – I understand since that the only *legal* obligation of a surety is the third: to see that the person gets to court. Yet this is supposed to be so heavy a responsibility that it takes the full resources of two people (where there are two signatures) to manage it. The irony of this in the face of caseloads of 60, 80, and 100 for probation or parole workers is absurd. Even parents somehow manage to raise more than one child at a time. Moreover, a person on bail is SUPPOSED still to be presumed innocent, and I always find references to controlling their behaviour a direct denial of this presumption.

Although our lawyer pressed him as far as possible, the JP remained adamant, and we had to leave a stunned and tearful Karen there. Nor did any of us feel a great deal better about the experience than she did.

Yet this was still not all. The farce or tragedy was reenacted with a different JP who had a different hard and fast rule that evening. Because we were so distressed at what had happened to Karen, we acted quickly. Ann Buttrick, who works with me and who already knew Karen personally, agreed to be her surety. Ann, Karen's boyfriend, and the lawyer returned to the Don that evening after assembling Ann's house deed and other necessaries. Again Karen was brought down, again her hopes were raised, and this time Ann was refused – because this JP considered that, for any property bail over $5000, Crown approval of the surety is required. Yet this was not stated anywhere on the bail order, nor are these rules printed on the walls of the Don for visitors to see and heed. I have personally seen cases where each has not been observed. The point is there is a great lack of clarity, which results in daily tragedies in our justice system.

Before this occasion, we had heard often from people we talked with from the rank and file of our jails, of relatives and friends arbitrarily turned down by JPs even for putting up small amounts of cash bail. Some will take bail from people out of the city, some won't. But this was our first direct experience with an attitude which seemed to be that the purpose of the JP was to keep as many in as possible, or at least to make the game as tough for relatives and friends to play out successfully as they could. For instance, it took Ann and the lawyer the better part of the next day to arrange the necessary Crown approval and make sure every possible loophole was covered before risking a third tragedy.

They were successful, but not all lower class people have these kinds of resources. If the system was this difficult for us as middle class people with a fair amount of experience with it, and the help of a capable and concerned lawyer, what must it be like for the distraught young wife and mother, trying to cope with the needs of her family and the confusing demands of a frightening system in which she suddenly finds her husband caught?

Another example will illustrate another problem. Recently a friend of ours was arrested on a minor charge on a Saturday morning. Two other good friends of his and I spent a good deal of time Monday phoning, trying to locate where he could be, since we were not sure on what charge or in what jurisdiction he was being held. Despite a cooperative and helpful response from the police and Don Jail and other officials we talked with, none of us were able to locate him by Monday afternoon, when we finally got a call through the Salvation Army from him, telling where he was and what bail was needed. Once again, if the three of us who were experienced with the system and calm about the situation had this much difficulty locating our friend, what must it be like for the inarticulate working class person whose nearest and dearest suddenly vanishes into the jaws of our justice system?

Since no computer system is perfect, the simplest solution to this latter problem is to allow several phone calls from a newly arrested person, to make sure he has a chance to tell those most concerned where he is and what is happening to him. Have you ever contemplated the fate of the person given one phone call who reaches a young child, a person who speaks another language than himself, a wrong number, or just one of those many indifferent people who fails to pass on messages?

Conclusions

Anyone reading this paper can draw his own conclusions, but here are a few which have struck me:

1) Rules for sureties must be CONSISTENT, CLEARLY POSTED IN JAILS, and REASONABLE. At present each JP seems to have his own set of rules, some of them unreasonable, and this results in a great deal of tragedy and frustration.

2) JPs should be trained for their job, and this training should include some concept that they are serving the public including relatives and friends of the incarcerated, and that their purpose is to administer fairly, not to be adjuncts of the custodial and punitive attitude toward accused persons.

3) Accused persons upon arrest should be allowed to make several calls as needed so that relatives can be properly informed.

4) Although I share the belief that a surety should have an ongoing, active, caring relationship with the person he goes bail for, the notion that a surety can only do this for one person at a time should be dispensed with for its patent absurdity, and the hardships it creates unnecessarily in the way of helping relationships which can be an aid to the community as well as the accused.

* * * * *

Writing this up a decade later, I still recall poignantly the look of bewilderment and shock on the face of Karen's fiance, the deep sharing of tears between Dianne, the lawyer and myself, and above all the rawness of Karen's pain. All these were set into glaring contrast by the brutal indifference of the JP. My comments about not understanding the motivation of a person who could apparently get satisfaction out of crushing Karen reflect my relative naivete at that time. Years of sad experience since have made me aware of the powerful force of vengeance in the human heart, which helps us deal with all our own guilt and anger by displacing it onto those we label "criminals," and feeling nothing is too bad for them. But one of my greatest contributions was my cheerful determination to attribute goodwill to all. My constant efforts to reach that of God in justice officials kept coming up against the realities of the system.

This led in January, 1979 to a major meeting with high officials, which was arranged by Margaret Campbell, the Liberals' Opposition Critic. Throughout this and some other struggles, Margaret was our strongest supporter. She had given up being a Judge in Family Court to try to be more effective through politics, and she was a formidable ally. I wrote the following report on the meeting for our Quaker Committee on Jails and Justice Newsletter:

MEETING WITH OFFICIALS ON BAIL PROBLEMS

Over the years we have been disturbed by inconsistencies and discourtesies of Justices of the Peace in deciding who is and is not fit to be surety. Although a certain amount of discretion is inevitable, the apparent total absence of consistent guidelines, the clear presence of class bias, the absence of any clear line of appeal against JP's decisions, long waits and discourtesies all frustrated us. Finally, after being turned down as a surety on the ground that I had already signed one other bail, but without finding any legal basis for this ground, I wrote a long letter to about 30 persons involved in the justice system. Out of the responses I got, the Minority Justice Critics of both NDP and the Liberal Party, Pat Lawlor and Margaret Campbell, arranged a meeting for us with the District Attorney's Office to discuss the problems.

Deputy Attorney General Allan Leal chaired the gathering, which included both Margaret Campbell and Pat Lawlor; Fred Franklin and myself representing AQCJJ; and Marlys Edwardh and Victor Paisley as defense lawyers we have found very informed, concerned, and helpful. In addition John Takach, Director of Crown Attorneys for Ontario, and Fred Hayes, Chief Judge, were present. It was a wonderful opportunity to meet with the people responsible for our justice system at the very top levels, and we deeply appreciated the excellent listening and free exchange.

Perhaps the most valuable function of the meeting was to establish communication lines between those running the system and concerned people who see the day to day problems. We felt these officials were disturbed by the stories we told them about absurd and arbitrary refusals, and we intend to keep sending them to them now once a month; we welcome contributions from readers of specific incidents.

Otherwise, some of the valuable things we learned were:

1)   There is no legal basis whatever for the one person to a surety ruling.

2)   JPs are responsible in various senses to all three of the officials named above. Judge Hayes is responsible for training them, but they derive their authority from the Crown's Office.

3)   In property bails, evidence of being able to pay from salary, savings or other non-property sources should be acceptable.

4)   There is a training manual for JPs but it is so secret even the Minority Justice Critics had trouble obtaining a copy.

5)   With sufficient further persuasion, they seemed open to eventually considering our plea for guidelines made available to the public, so that one has some idea where one stands. We also discussed judicial appeal, which the lawyers doubted would work, and legislative remedies.

I included a list of officials to write to about further bail problems, and I closed with the following quote:

'The rich, moneyed man who makes his riches by exploitation or other questionable means is no less guilty of robbery than the thief. The only difference is that the former takes refuge behind a facade of respectability, and escapes the penalty of the law.

'Strictly speaking, all amassing or hoarding of wealth above and beyond one's legitimate requirements is theft. There would be no occasion for thefts and therefore no thieves if there was a wise regulation of riches, and absolute social justice prevailed."

— Gandhi

*   *   *   *   *

I also sent the following letter to all the officials who attended the meeting. I am including all the positive comments and the summary of details to indicate how meticulously I tried to do all the work of a positive, constructive volunteer, working to support whatever could be supported while trying to change the unthinkable and immoral.

January 28, 1979

We want to thank all of you for your time in arranging and attending the meeting January 16th in Deputy Attorney General Leal's board room on the questions raised in my letter on "bails and JP's." We appreciated not only the time, but the quality of listening and sharing at the meeting. Every lawyer we called beforehand about the meeting who knew anything about Mr. Leal commented on his basic commitment to fair play. We came away with a similar impression about all participants, in their fundamental desire for fair play in the justice system.

As I mentioned at the end of the meeting, my main remaining concern is regarding follow-up. It was certainly valuable for us to have a better understanding of those who are directing our justice system at the highest levels. I trust it was also useful to you to get our perspective on some of the problems we see at the grassroots level. It is almost impossible for those at the top of any system to be fully informed of the experience of consumers at the day-to-day level.

To review briefly a few examples of specific problems and practices that have disturbed us, out of a wider variety we have known:

1)   ONE PERSON - ONE BAIL RULING. On two specific occasions I have been turned down as a surety SOLELY on this basis. On both occasions the JP stated specifically that he was not concerned with my financial or personal capability as a surety, but solely with my being surety for one other person. I understand from our meeting that this is not, by itself, an acceptable criterion.

2)   PASSPORT SURRENDER STANDS IN WAY.
In two specific cases we know of, JPs refused to release a person on bail because the order said he was to surrender his passport, and he did not have it at the jail.

3)   REDUCTION HEARING IN PROGRESS.
As mentioned in our discussion, in one recent case two extremely reliable sureties (one a social worker, one a priest, both well acquainted with the person to be bailed) were refused although prepared to go the full bail because proceedings were underway for a reduction in bail.

4)   REASONABLE CRITERIA TAKEN AS ABSOLUTE CATEGORICAL EXCLUSIONS.
I mentioned the case of our friend Bill Lewis, who had a conviction 8 years ago, has been completely clear ever since, runs a small agency of his own, and was refused categorically as a $500 surety for a friend because of his record.

These and other similar cases illustrate the kinds of experiences that concern us. I felt one of the most vital parts of our discussion centered around possible remedies for problems. A remedy for the occasional extreme abuse or error is vital to insure good general practice for all. Remedies discussed either at the meeting or in my letter include:

1)   JUDICIAL APPEAL.
Although most lawyers we have talked with seem very skeptical whether this is a realistic option, we intend to pursue this if possible, with an appropriate case.

2)   RECORDING OF JP-SURETY INTERVIEWS.
Having these interviews recorded, even on an experimental basis would give you some firsthand feedback on what goes on in the typical JP-surety interview, would be useful to you in training JPs, and would, we believe, cut down many of the large and small abuses and errors.

3)   ADMINISTRATIVE GUIDELINES FOR JPs, AVAILABLE TO PUBLIC.
We still feel these will be extremely useful, and an improvement to make practice more consistent and understandable. When I hear of the difficulties the most experienced lawyers dealing with bailings encounter, still having to seek additional papers and steps, I am awestruck at the formidable task facing the average uninformed relative or friend trying to bail, who knows nothing whatever of the system and is in some fear of it.

4)   LEGISLATION.
Legislative remedy may be appropriate to clarify some particularly muddy areas.

We will appreciate further information from you on steps to deal with bail problems, and we intend to continue to keep you informed of the bail system as we experience it. At the risk of sounding like "some of my best friends are..." I do want to point out that we have had some very satisfying encounters with JPs who were courteous and helpful, well informed, and good translators of the law into practice. We would like to work with you toward making their practice more the general rule.

*   *   *   *   *

At first it appeared to us that our political system was working. Ed Ziemba, an NDP politician, in cooperation with the two Major Justice Critics, brought our bail concerns to the Justice Committee of the Provincial Parliament. Julie Hoffman, dynamic Director of the Family and Friends (of prisoners) Agency across from the Don Jail, joined me in testifying to all the major ills of surety abuse and inconsistent, unjust JP rulings. The Attorney General's representative at the hearing went on record in Hansard that the one person – one bail ruling was not valid or legal. We were heard very sympathetically, great concern was expressed over the discourtesies of JPs, and follow-up was promised. Two specific amendments were drafted into the new legislation, making clear sureties were not to be turned down merely because they had another person on bail, and stating that sureties are only responsible for getting the person to court, not for his other behaviour.

Cold reality set in gradually. The promised follow-up did not occur, and we gradually discovered JPs continued to do what they pleased, for there was no consistent check on their absolute power to accept or reject sureties. The first test of this came in March, when I attempted to follow the suggestions made to date, phoning Chief Judge Hayes about an apparent abuse.

His position which he later put in writing, simply confirmed the lack of appeal: he refused to intervene now or ever, and did not feel anyone else should. Still trying hard to be positive, but firm, I wrote the following letter to all the officials and community people we had been working with on these issues:

March 19, 1979

I am writing about further steps on the problems of sureties. I hope you do not feel that we have a fixation in this area, or are unappreciative of the enormous progress that has been made through your help. It is precisely because we recognize that progress and appreciate it that we feel that it is essential to build on it; the progress that has been made enables us to pinpoint and move toward the next steps which will make sure of more equal justice before the law in regard to acceptance of sureties.

Last week I got a complaint on a turndown, by way of Family and Friends Centre. Briefly, Douglas Muir needed a $500 no deposit bail to get out of the Don, or he would lose his job. His pregnant wife brought a mutual friend, Sandra Dutrizac, to the jail to bail out Douglas Muir. Ms. Dutrizac had a bank account with $500, owned a car, and is employed with a steady job. She brought evidence of all these, but was turned down, supposedly on financial grounds. As I understand it, the JP insisted that since her means were somewhat limited, he was going to protect her interests by refusing to allow her to take this risk.

We had been told to phone the Attorney General's Office with complaints, should we receive them. Because of the situation of this young family, with the wife pregnant and the husband's job in jeopardy, I tried to phone about this one. I was referred very courteously through a number of offices to Judge Hayes. He was good enough to call me at 5 p.m. as he was leaving for the day.

His basic position, as I understand it, was that neither he nor I knew certain facts, which was true enough, and so he would not "second guess an independent officer of the judiciary." He thought the JP might have really turned the woman down because he doubted her ability to see that the man got to court. But as the JP did not say this, this conjecture opens up the possibility that we can always assume a reasonable ground may have existed when a person is turned down on an unreasonable one.

Also, if a JP's decision is so independent as not to be subject to review by anyone, he is more independent than a Judge. I do not mean to put too much weight on Judge Hayes' spontaneous remarks without discussing his position further with him, but insofar as I did understand them, they have helped pinpoint for me precisely what seems needed in this area.

Until we have an objective list of grounds for rejection, we have no rule of law; and until there is some record of the reason for rejection, there is no possibility of reasonable review. All the laws in the world can have little effect, because the JP, if he operates totally beyond review or appeal, operates beyond the rule of law.

Therefore, I feel we need the following:

1) A LIST OF REASONS FOR REJECTING SURETIES.

If we had a list of the reasons why sureties can be rejected, we would have a much clearer basis for understanding decisions, preparing sureties, and knowing what is just in this area. Without such a list, one can always speculate that possibly a JP had something reasonable in mind.

2) A PAPER GIVEN TO REJECTED SURETIES BY EACH JP.

This paper, a copy of which would be kept by the JP also, would state the names of all parties including the JP, date, the category of rejection, and briefly why this surety fell into the category in the JP's judgement.

3)   SOME AUTHORITY FOR REVIEW,
to whom a surety could go with this paper.

Until we have something along these lines, I feel we will be stymied in implementing the concerns we share in this area. The Douglas Muirs will remain incarcerated, because there is no way of appealing such decisions, or of knowing enough about their basis TO appeal them. I am told that some JPs are making a habit of denying all sureties who come to bail out accused persons who were on probation at the time of the new charge, because they believe such persons should not be out, whether given bail by the court or not. If this is so, it illustrates that the final authority JPs can exercise exceeds that of the courts.

I would like very much to discuss this with you further and also strategies for changing this situation. I realize some of these problems border on matters beyond what legislation can rectify, but feel you have been so helpful thus far, your advice and assistance on how to proceed further would be most valuable. We would also welcome from you more information on how we can work more effectively with the existing structure to make constructive changes. May I ask you to invite appropriate members of the government, if you feel it appropriate at this point?

I have written several enthusiastic reports about the progress in this area so far, which have gone out to Canadian Friends Service Committee AQCJJ, and the Defense Lawyers' Periodical. The enclosed report is one of these, and I can only repeat the appreciation expressed therein for your excellent work.

*   *   *   *   *

Ironically, the very next day after this letter was written, I had another excruciating experience in bailing someone out. Although some of the issues may seem rather petty, the experience of waiting hours and then having others put before one is yet one more illustration of the mistreatment of sureties. By this time I was familiar with the need to document carefully while the experience was fresh, so I wrote out the following detailed account:

AN EXPERIENCE IN BAILING – March 20, 1979

While doing my volunteer work at Toronto West Detention Centre, I met a couple in their late 40's who had never been charged with any offence before, and who had four grown children, and a lifetime of employment without trouble, and owned a home of their own. The charges against them had to do with sexual offences all in the confines of their own home; the serious ones in my view involved the accusation of corruption of two boys. Both denied this charge, but whether valid or not, after talking with them, I was convinced they were sufficiently traumatized to observe any terms of bail scrupulously, and that the community's best interest as well as theirs would be to get them out as soon as possible. In the course of exploring the matter, I always talk to other people to check out facts and references, and in this case I spoke to their lawyer, the jail chaplain, and the 22-year-old son of the couple, a very responsible young man who was doing his best to cope with a very difficult situation.

On Tuesday, March 20, I dedicated the day to getting them out on bail. I think it is illuminating to note that I was out of the house 11 hours, during only 4 of which I was doing anything other than working on this bail. I phoned the Crown's Office the day before, but found it impossible to make an appointment, so came at 10 in the morning with the 22-year-old son, "Mark." Mark only owned cars as property, and the bails were $3500 each, Crown approved, so it was uncertain whether he could bail them out. Neither the lawyer nor he realized that his substantial income as a salesman for automotive parts might constitute acceptable proof as a surety on a non-cash bail.

I encouraged Mark to come with me in the hope that he could be surety for one parent, and I for the other, or at the least, the show of family solidarity would carry some further weight with the Crown. Mark was very well dressed, well spoken, mature for his age, and ironically his ambition was to move from his sales work into joining the police force.

We waited till nearly noon when a Crown arrived, who was courteous, professional, and efficient. The Crown decided he preferred a professional outsider as surety for both, so approved me as a surety for husband and wife, and Mark and I went on our ways. I had to teach at a community college in the afternoon, but at 4:15 p.m. I arrived at Toronto West with all possible papers: the Crown approvals, proper identification, our house deed, and savings certificates.

Theoretically, it should have been easy, short, and almost automatic at this point. The guard on duty at reception was a particularly helpful and efficient man who knows me well and he phoned the central JP's number to tell the JP there was a surety waiting with all papers in order. The JP was supposed to return the call, saying how long it would be before he could get there. The man at the desk said sometimes they refuse to come back till evening, but if so, he could tell me, in which case I could go home and have dinner, and come back.

In fact, the call was never returned. In another hour, he placed another call with the same message, and there was still no return. At 6 p.m., a second person arrived to bail someone out, but still no JP. Finally at 7:15 p.m., the JP arrived. But as has happened to me once before at Toronto West, the 6 p.m. arrival, who had waited 1 and 3/4 hours less, was seen first. So I waited till 8 p.m., NEARLY FOUR HOURS FROM ARRIVAL, before I saw a JP, a Mr. McCurd, I understand from the man at reception.

It is not always easy to learn from anyone the name of the JP you are dealing with, which is a very serious flaw in the system, in my opinion. Recently, when Family and Friends had a problem with the JP, and asked officially for his name, the man at the desk at the Don Jail flatly refused to reveal it. It is rarely revealed in the interview, and to ask in the atmosphere created often seems an act of hostility which requires daring, since the JP has the absolute power to refuse what you want, and can get only through him/her.

Mr. McCurd asked me a series of questions, including whether I had anyone else on bail. I answered that I had one other at present, and he was doing well. He wondered if the Crown knew this, and asked a number of other questions in a critical vein, concluding with, "Do you think it is a good thing you do, coming in here as a volunteer and bailing people out, because I'll tell you, if you didn't have Crown approval, I would reject you as a surety."

At this point, I struggled to retain my temper, which the long hours of waiting had exacerbated, and responded with: "Do you think it is a good thing you do, seeing someone first who has been waiting 1 and 3/4 hours less? Would you like it if your doctor handled his patients that way?" He answered accurately that that had nothing to do with his question to me, and I acknowledged this, but said I'd like to discuss both.

He then said he did not establish the order in which he saw people; this was done by the jail. Yet when I had questioned the guard at the desk the other time it had happened to me, he told me he gave the list in the order they arrived, and the JP decided what order to see them. Either there is a middle man (possibly the jail's bail clerk) messing things up, or someone is not being truthful. One of the difficulties is that one is caught between the jail bureaucracy and the JP, and it is hard for me to know where the problem lies in some cases. For this reason, I am submitting this report to the jail, as well as to the people I have been reporting JP problems to.

At this point I said, "Look, if I am snarky, it is because I missed lunch AND dinner today working on this bail, and have been waiting four hours to see you." He said he had never received a call from Toronto West until 6:20 p.m. Since he had a walkie-talkie on him, either again the man at the desk was lying, which I think very unlikely, or the JP was lying (a possibility I can't assess, not knowing him), or again, someone in the middle who is supposed to pass on calls failed to do so for either the 4:15 or the 5:15 follow-up call.

The JP now began to identify with my situation, saying he knew how it was to miss meals because of work, and came out with a list of his own complaints about pressure of work. We entered a period of armed camaraderie, and I felt he was more courteous after I had snapped back at him. I did discuss his concern about my bailing, explaining I only bailed a few, and gave them good supervision; but I left without any assurance he would approve me, should I again approach him in a few months, because of his feelings about two bails to a customer, and about my status as a volunteer. Thanks to the activities of our friends in the legislature and in the Attorney General's Office, I can wave Hansard at him, but in the last analysis, IF HE SAYS NO, I HAVE NO APPEAL.

What this case illustrates is, I think:

1)   Unconscionable delays, impossible for me to trace between the jail and the JP.

2)   The absolute power of the JP in the surety situations makes the bias some have toward keeping as many in as possible insurmountable. This contrasts sharply with new proposals from the Department of Corrections itself for community bail supervision by people like myself, recognizing that it is in the community's best interests even to pay us to supervise responsibly many kinds of people waiting for trial. It also contrasts sharply with the understanding I have met with whenever I have approached a Crown about approval as a surety.

The second is, in my opinion, the more serious problem. Although the frustrations and delays described here may seem a trivial waste of your time, I thought it might be useful to have a case history of some of the minor problems sureties encounter, as well as the major issue raised again on whether the surety is approved.

* * * * *

Less than two weeks later, I was apprised of a circumstance which added further light to the refusal of sureties, for it was such a clear proof of the arbitrary nature of the decisions. I called it a controlled study, because a surety was turned down for inadequate financial ability for a $500 bail, who soon after was accepted by another JP for a $1000 bail.

FOOTNOTE ON BAIL: "A Controlled Study"
April 3, 1979

One recent experience illustrates the inconsistency we have complained of. March 5, Sandra Carson approached the JP on duty at the Don Jail in the afternoon, whose name we were unable to obtain from the desk afterwards. She wished to be surety for Douglas Muir, who needed a $500 no-deposit bail, and who was about to lose his job, and had a pregnant wife to support. Ms. Carson was refused as a surety by the JP, supposedly on financial grounds, although she showed a bankbook with $500 in it, ownership of a car, and was employed. The JP seemed to feel he should protect her from taking this risk with her limited financial means. I phoned Judge Hayes' office about this, but he felt he could not review the decision without knowing more about it; I can sympathize with his dilemma, but it illustrates the impossibility of review or appeal at present.

Less than two weeks later the same surety, Ms. Carson, approached another JP on duty at the Don Jail for another friend of hers, Wayne Roy, equally well known to her, and who needed a $1000 no-deposit bond. She was accepted without question. She phoned us to let us know, and I think it is a rather clear illustration of the problem.

The surety was the same person, in the same financial position, and with the same degree of knowledge of the person to be bailed. Only two things could have varied: the nature of the person to be bailed, and the views of the JP handling it. Surely it is not the prerogative of a JP to determine that some persons who have been granted bail by a court are unworthy to be bailed, so I find either possibility unacceptable.

* * * * *

A week later I was writing to the officials again about an outrageous experience my husband had with a JP who took it into his head that all sureties must have Crown approval:

REGARDING BAILS AND JPs
April 11, 1979

Here is some further data on bailing problems. I don't mean to bury you in it, but every time I resolve to leave it alone for awhile, fresh material comes to hand to remind us that thus far, nothing has improved.

Last week my husband tried to bail someone out of the Don whom he knew – Ray has only signed one bail before in his life. He had the house deed with him, and Ray's regular income is several times per month the proposed no-deposit bail of $1000. Yet the JP, Patrick Deakin, insisted, after close questioning revealed he could have no objection to Ray as a surety, that Ray go over and obtain Crown approval for this bail. He explained that the Crown functions like a bank, to doublecheck the house deed and anything else financial, and you have to see the JP before and after. He was polite, but absolutely adamant, and since he was only at the Don from 2-4, it was impossible for anyone to complete a bail under his jurisdiction in the afternoon. Ray managed to see the Crown, who said he was the seventh person Mr. Deakin had sent his way that day, and he had been trying to reach him all day without success to stop the ridiculous flow on small bails. The jail did not admit Ray or one other who arrived back about 5 p.m. to bail, and fortunately there was a library nearby for shelter. This bail also was not completed till 8:30 p.m., a total working time of 6 hours, involving considerable persistence. As long as Mr. Deakin is on duty afternoons at the Don, I see no point in people trying to bail then, since by the time they see the Crown after him, they will have to come back to the night JP who doesn't insist on this uniform Crown approval.

I appreciated Margaret Campbell's two letters, and trust that the changes necessary are going to be forthcoming. Until we have a system of SOMETHING IN WRITING TO REJECTED SURETIES and SOME FORM OF APPEAL FROM JP'S RULINGS, I don't think anything will improve.

Thanks again to all of you for the time you have put in. I am ready to meet with anyone any time to further improvements in this area. I look forward to action.

*   *   *   *   *

At this point, events began to impede the progress we thought we were making, despite the repeated problems. We were told to await developments of a committee that was working on the issues we had raised, and we met with a stone wall as far as any review of individual JP rulings. At the same time, I was approached to head up the new Toronto Bail Program, in which role I would be given considerable power to alleviate on a larger scale many bail inequities. This forcibly diverted my energies. However, two months after I began the Bail Program, I made another attempt to address the problems constructively, using the new Bail Program to build better communication and structures:

November 5, 1979

Dear Friends,

Last year we had several meetings and a good deal of correspondence over questions I raised about the consistency of Justice of the Peace in approving sureties in the signing of bails. Some progress was certainly made in airing of the issue, in testifying to the legislative committee on it, and in specific amendments that were pertinent. I am writing partly to ask about further progress, which was to be reported as I understood it this fall, after there was time for more study of the problems.

But I am also writing in my new capacity as Project Manager for the Old City Hall Bail Project. As part of this project, we have workers now located in Toronto West Detention Centre, and the Toronto Jail. We will have someone from the Bail Project in Toronto East Detention Centre in about two weeks. In making arrangements for the project to operate in these jails, institutional staff in the two institutions spontaneously asked us, believe it or not, for help in dealing with frustrations between JPs and potential sureties. It seems to me that having regular staff in the jails concerned with bails offers us an opportunity to try a creative experiment to deal with some of the problems we have discussed.

Jail personnel argued that when sureties are being turned down en masse or on grounds they are unprepared for, or sent home for papers they could have brought had they known, the resultant frustrations explode on the jail personnel as well as the Justice of the Peace. The following proposal made sense to all those at the planning meetings:

1)   That the general handbook for JPs instructions on accepting or rejecting sureties be made available to bail workers in the Jails.

2)   That a short meeting be held between each new JP coming on rotation at a jail and the bail worker, to clarify understanding on who is and is not an acceptable surety and what documentation must be brought.

3)   That any points of difference in their mutual understanding, should such occur, be taken to some appropriate authority, such as Judge Hayes or Mr. Takach or persons appointed by them. This would avoid unnecessary complications in many cases.

4)   With such mutual understanding established, the bail workers would then function to assist in informing sureties of what they should bring, and would try to do a little initial screening of bail prospects so that those who came were most likely to be reasonably appropriate and prepared. They should be able to assist both the JP and the surety in minimizing frustrations.

I hope to hear from you regarding this possibility, and any other news you may have of progress in facilitating consistency on surety questions. Recently I was myself involved in a bailing where the court had named the father of the accused in the amount of $5000 as a surety, but the JP interpreted it that the father should have gotten Crown approval, apart from the Court's naming him as an acceptable surety. The argument that the Crown was fully represented in Court and had adequate opportunity to approve or disapprove then carried no weight. This is one of the areas of unclarity where greater clearness would certainly be useful.

Jail personnel noted, as I have too, that some JPs require Crown approval of all sureties, however small the bail, and that the resulting confusion and time consumption creates bad feelings between potential sureties and the jail; it also usually frustrates the Crown's Office because of time spent by them. In another instance reported by a prisoner at Mimico, a bail surety was refused because the paper said "the bondsman shall..." and the surety was not, of course, a professional bondsman!

In any case, I hope the experiment proposed above may alleviate some of the problems, and be a help to all parties. I look forward to hearing from you about the idea.

*   *   *   *   *

None of the above things happened, and the only apparent effect of my years of patient and constructive work on the subject was that those JPs who were aware of my testimony on the topic, held it against me. Accordingly, swept up in the new program, I turned my energies toward what I could do in that way. But periodically I was reminded again of the running score of JP's arbitrary rulings with sureties. A particularly painful case was brought to my attention in April of 1980, and I reported on it in a letter to Margaret Campbell:

April 19, 1980

Dear Margaret,

Turning to our old favourite subject, bails and JPs, which I am sure we are both tired of, if only one could see movement...thanks very much for your letter and the one from the Attorney General. Recently in doing a task I ran over the fact that the JPs' powers go back to the 14th century, so felt a little better that a few years' work on some of the problems accumulated over the centuries hasn't yet made much visible inroads on those problems. Nonetheless, seriously I think the enclosed case history which I will explain more fully here illustrates that we are still in the dark ages in this area.

With regard to Mr. McMurty's letter, I am delighted that finally someone has received a response after so many months. But among the outstanding questions remaining are the following:

1)   He speaks of further meetings between me and various persons. I have been invited to no such meetings, and know of no action being pursued on the subject. Last spring I was told steps were being taken and I would be contacted in the fall about their results, but I can only assume this has been lost sight of.

2)   Where is the remedy for persons such as Mr. Culp and his several frustrated would-be sureties?

3)   I see no response yet to my specific requests for the JPs to put something in writing, and for there to be a clear process of appeal known to sureties, and for there to be publicly available guidelines for sureties to know what JPs should expect.

Now, with regard to Mr. Culp and Mr. Coupe, here is the background:

On Friday, April 18, Brian Coupe entered my office, seeking help from the Bail Project for his friend, Wayne Culp. Brian had met me at Mimico as part of our Quaker volunteer program there, so knew about my role in the Project and sought me out accordingly.

Brian said that he and Wayne Culp had a record for robbery, finished serving their time at Mimico in October, got jobs and had been working and sharing a house with other friends since then. Recently, Brian received an income tax refund, cashed it, and made the mistake of showing some of the money in a public place.

On Sunday, April 13, in the morning, two strangers jumped Brian when Wayne was with him. One of them struck Brian on the forehead with a weapon which opened a wide gash, requiring seven stitches later to close. The two would-be robbers also threatened Brian and Wayne with a large stick if they didn't hand over Brian's money, but they ran away instead. Brian hailed a police car, which stopped, but probably because of their record, Brian and Wayne ended up charged with robbery by the two would-be thieves. Moreover, they were taken to Station 14, where Brian was beaten further by the police, opening his wound wider, till he passed out and required hospitalization. Perhaps because they were alarmed over his condition, Brian felt, the police then released Brian from the hospital on his own recognizance, but Wayne remained in custody till Monday morning, when he had bail of $1000 set at 10 a.m. in Court 23. From there the story goes on as I have typed it on the next two pages.

I have nothing but Brian's word for the foregoing, but he says he can produce a photostat of the income tax refund and a number of witnesses to state that he had just received this money to prove it was his. He is charging the police with assault. I would be glad to see if I could get him together with you or anyone else you think would be interested, because the whole story is rather appalling, as I think you will agree, and Brian is a very effective reporter – you can make your own judgments from there.

Thanks for all your marvellous human concern, Margaret. I look forward to hearing from you further.

Details:

Saturday night, Sunday morning, April 13 – arrested at 10:30 a.m.

Brian Coupe released that afternoon, 3 p.m., on promise to appear.

Wayne Culp held for show cause hearing Monday, April 14th. (Court 23 – 10 a.m.) Given $1000 bail, one signature.

After court at City Hall Frazer McWhinnie went to City Hall JP after 1/2 hour wait. Asked for proof of $1000. Brought out bank hook with $470 savings account, ownership for $2000 motorcycle, and ownership for $1000 stereo, both new. Also said had been working 1 1/2 years for Griffin House Graphics, making $350 per week, $9 per hour. The JP told him he would have to have $1000 in the bank. If he could find a friend with that in the bank or if he could put that in the bank he would be willing to let him out, no problem.

Surety was denied, and Frazer left.

Next, Frazer withdrew money from his account, phoned his commonlaw wife at work and asked her to borrow $600 on her chargex card. Then deposited $1000 in bank at Yonge and St. Clair, and got a bank statement stating that at the close of the day Zita Hoare had a balance of $1147. This was Monday night.

Monday night she went to the JP at the Don, Mr. Deacon.

Zita: "I'd like to bail out Wayne Culp."

JP: "Do you have something to show me for surety in the amount of $1000?"

Zita: "I have a bank statement." (She gave it to him.)

JP: "Do you have your bank book?"

Zita: "No, I didn't think that would be any good as proof." (Book not updated by bank.)

JP: "Well, how do I know you didn't just put it in the bank today. I need to see something to know you've not just put it in."

Zita: "Well, my paycheque goes right into the bank…"

JP: "Why do you have a chequeing account instead of a savings account where you could get interest?"

Zita: ….

JP: "He has quite a few serious charges. I need more than a bank statement. Where do you work?" (In fact, he had only one charge.)

Zita: "Imperial Life, Yonge and St. Clair."

JP: "Do you have anything to show how long you've worked there?"

Zita: "A few pay stubs for last month."

JP: "That doesn't show me how long you've worked there. I need to have a letter from your employer. Can you get one?"

Zita: "Yes."

JP: "Well, I suggest you come back tomorrow with a letter from your employer. I'm here at 2 and 7."

Zita: "I need a letter from my employer and my bankbook."

JP: "Well, the letter from your employer."

Zita: "I'll be in at 7 tomorrow."

Frazer: (Swears as leaving.)

End of 14th.

April 15, Tuesday

As JP enters jail, seeing Zita waiting.

JP: "Did you bring that guy with you tonight?"

Zita: "No."

JP: "Who was he?"

Zita: "A friend. We had been waiting two hours. He was just upset."

Zita is called in a few minutes later. Benches piled up and a few men washing floors, water on floor.

JP: "Did you bring that letter?"

Zita: "Yes." She produced bank statement.

JP: "I don't want to see that." (Puts down, gives work letter.)

JP: "If you had brought your friend with you, I wouldn't have let you bail this man out." (Gets out form, asking name, address.)

JP: (To girl) – "Bring Wayne Culp down." (Which she did.)

JP: "Step aside while I do someone else." (She does.)

Called back, Wayne standing there.

JP: "Is this him?"

Zita: "Yes."

JP: "Do you know her?"

Wayne: "Yes."

JP: "What's her name?"
Wayne: "Zita."
JP: "What's her last name?"
Wayne: "I can't remember."
JP: "Do you know where she lives?"
Wayne: "Bathurst and Davenport, 633."
JP: "How long has she lived there?"
Wayne: "About a week."
JP: "You don't know her last name?"
Wayne: "I can't remember, she's married." (Commonlaw) "Her husband's name is Frazer McWhinnie…"
JP: "But you don't know her maiden name. Well, I can't do this, you don't know her well enough. If that was her husband last night, I can't let him out to you because his conduct was really bad. I could charge him with…"
Zita: "And also I've got this letter from the Crown Attorney."
JP: "I'm in charge here. I don't want to see it."
One more person comes in.
JP: "Well, I'll do him, but I won't do any more. I'm in an inch of water and can't hear any more."

Wednesday – different JP in afternoon – turned down because he said she had already been there twice. She had Crown approval Tuesday and Wednesday, and Deacon refused to look at it; second JP looked at it, kept it, and refused to return it.

* * * * *

Margaret replied with her customary warmth and promptness, saying in part: "Really, it's a horror story, you're quite right. I will bring it up at the estimates…I'm so tired of batting my head against this kind of a brick wall, and I am sure you are too, but hang in there and I'll hang in here and we'll see if between us we can't make some dint in this situation. God bless…"

I continued to document abuses from time to time, but there seemed little response, and none of the reforms I suggested was acted upon. I made one more major effort to address them. In 1980, partly in my office as Director of the Bail Program, I was invited to testify to an Interministerial Committee on pretrial issues. I devoted much of my testimony to JPs and their treatment of sureties. In it I summed up much of my experience over the years.

INTERMINISTERIAL COMMITTEE
Presentation by Ruth Morris

Justices Of The Peace and Signing Of Bails With Approved Sureties

I am devoting a major portion of my testimony to this area because it is in my opinion a very major issue in the system, and problem. I speak out of years of experience as a concerned Quaker volunteer, as well as in my new role as Director of the Bail Program, Toronto-York. I think any serious attempt to evaluate the problems of remand prisoners must re-examine the whole role of the surety, and of the Justice of the Peace in determining who is and is not acceptable as a surety. Three demands I have been making for several years still seem reasonable to me, and I repeat them here:

1)   CLEAR, PUBLICLY AVAILABLE GUIDELINES FOR JPs
on who is acceptable. I have heard intimations that there are such guidelines, but have never been able to obtain a copy. If they exist, but are secret, how can sureties know what documentation to provide? Surely the essence of any justice is that the parties involved know the standards by which they are judged.

2)   SOMETHING IN WRITING FROM JPs
on each rejection, stating the general reason for rejection, so the surety has some basis for understanding the decision, and also for appeal where it is unjust.

3)   CLEAR SYSTEM FOR APPEAL.
Judges' decisions, made by officials with higher levels of training and authority, have a definite appeal procedure and right. Not so JP's rulings on sureties. Although some lawyers believe in theory appeal may be possible, the possibility is so obscure it has never been done. Until there is a form of appeal for sureties, the rule of law will not exist in this area.

HISTORY

In the course of the last several years, I have become interested in the problems of sureties, partly from meeting a number of

69

frustrated and distraught relatives of prisoners, and partly from being a surety myself in a number of cases. The following is only a partial list of the cases I have personally become aware of, as I began to keep a record only after many incidents had made me conscious of it, and still have many other interests which prevent me from documenting all cases I happen to hear of.

1)   Early 1977. When Julie Hoffman (Director of Family and Friends at that time) had already been accepted as a surety, a comment indicated she had bailed someone before. The JP said, "You could be prosecuted as a bail bondsman," and intimated she was making a profit. Ms. Hoffman adds, "Anyone ignorant of the system would have been intimidated. His attitude was certainly threatening."

2)   October 12, 13, 1977, from Bert Ross, volunteer probation officer in Newmarket area, 26 May Ave., Sharm, Ontario, L0G 1V0. Waited till 2 a.m. at Don Jail for JP to bail boy out for $200 no-deposit bail. Was then told he had to show him $200 before the 17-year-old could be released, despite ample identification on his work and role as volunteer probation officer. Returned October 13 with $200 and after waiting till 3 a.m., did bail the boy out, took him home.

3)   Mid November, 1977. Ms. Hoffman attempted to post bail. C.O. at jail informed JP she was already surety for another person, and JP refused to accept her. Ms. Hoffman argued the two bails together totalled $1500 and she had with her the deed to her house, value $56,000. He still refused.

4)   November 15-23, 1977. Following other complications on an appeal bail, I was told I could not sign as the second person on this bail since I had someone else on bail, but my husband could.

5)   Late November, a Sunday, 1977, P. Taggett. JP first tried to refuse on money grounds, then the surety showed him deeds to a cottage in her purse. Then told "Even JP Taylor couldn't get him out because of lack of control over him." Also said knowledge of him for only three months was insufficient.

6)   On two separate occasions in 1978 and 1979 I was rejected as a surety because I had one other person on bail at the time. On both occasions the JP made it very clear that was the only reason, and that he was not even interested in any other considerations such as whether I was financially or personally capable of supervising more than one person at a time. The first was May of 1978 for a Native woman, the second was for Al Bellefeuille. Both were at the Don Jail, but with different JPs.

7)   Julie Hoffman and a Priest were rejected as sureties for someone because his bail was under appeal for reduction although they expressed willingness to bail him out at the full amount! (1978)

8)   March 5, 1979. Sandra Carson attempted to bail Douglas Muir at Don Jail, $500 bail. He was about to lose his job and had a pregnant wife. Ms. Carson, a friend of the family was refused on financial grounds, although she showed a bankbook with $500 in it, ownership of a car, and she was employed.

Less than two weeks later, Ms. Carson attempted to bail another friend. Wayne Roy, equally long relationship, needed a $1000 bond. She was accepted without question, with the same credentials.

An attempt to appeal the ruling immediately on Douglas Muir through Judge Hayes was wholly unsuccessful. He basically does not feel it a function of his to question the decision of a JP.

9)   March 20, 1979. As a volunteer at Toronto West Detention Centre, I attempted to bail a couple in their late 40's with a grown family and a lifetime without criminal charges. Although I got Crown approval as surety without much difficulty except the expenditure of about four hours, I waited four hours at the jail before the JP even saw me. He saw another person before me who had arrived nearly two hours after I did. Taking people out of order is another common discourtesy of JPs. JP began with an attack, "Do you think it is a good thing you do, coming in here as a volunteer and bailing people out, because I'll tell you, if you didn't have Crown approval, I would reject you as a surety." With patience I did succeed in the bailing despite this beginning.

10)   December 24, 1979. Frank Showler, Coordinator of Canadian Friends Service Committee, was rejected for a $500 bail for a prisoner at Toronto East Detention Center because the JP felt only the mother could control the prisoner. The mother had terminal cancer and was too ill to come down to bail. Despite the explanation and the date, the prisoner stayed in jail for Christmas and the surety was rejected. Frank owns a $70,000 home without other liabilities, and is a very responsible person, recently retired from a government job.

11)   Spring, 1980. Two brothers in Don Jail. Parents come to bail both, told by JP they will have to choose which one. The one not chosen reacts badly, crushed that parents bailed his brother and left him. Reported by Bail Project Staff.

12)   April 13, 1980. Wayne Culp held on $1000 bail, no deposit. I have written a graphic account verbatim of this series of encounters in which:

1)   First surety, Frazer, rejected at courthouse for financial reasons though he showed ownership of new stereo and motorcycle, bankbook with $470 and stated had been working 1 1/2 years for Griffin House Graphics, making $350 a week, $9 an hour. Told he had to produce a bankbook with at least $1000 in it and then he could be surety, no matter if someone put it in immediately for him.

2)   Second surety, Frazer's commonlaw wife, Zita, borrowed money on her chargex card to fill her bank account over $1000. Got bank statement giving balance at close of day $1147. JP wants bankbook, which is not updated by bank regularly. JP argues about merits of savings vs. chequing account. Says accused has several serious charges (in fact only one) so he needs more than bank statement. Paystubs not enough, wants letter from employer.

3)   Zita returns, next night, with bankbook and letter from employer. Accused person called down, interrogated on surety's name, address, length of residence.

Rejected because although he knows her married name and address and length of residence, he doesn't know her maiden name. Surety tries to show Crown Approval letter, JP says, "I don't want to see it."

4) Surety Zita returns next day to different JP, but JP aware she has been turned down and he also refuses to consider Crown Approval letter and turns her down.

5) On weekend, accused's parents drive in from country and after some difficulty, succeed in bailing him.

13) August 25, 1980. Surety Herman Murphy rejected in trying to post bail for Tom McCaskell, $1000 no-deposit bail. Surety has bankbook with over $1000 showing, part-ownership in grocery store, owns two small lots of rural land and is employed at St. Michael's Detox Centre at $14,000 per year. He has known accused for 12 years. Surety has a criminal record for drink-related offences, but has been dry and employed for about 4 years. Rejection reason unclear, but apparently on basis of the surety having gone to the trouble of arranging accommodation and job when court order required another plan. Surety immediately accepted court order plan when told this, but JP not satisfied, JP also argued that if accused in three weeks, might as well leave him, and that accused not worth it.

* * * * *

The above is only a partial catalogue of the instances I am aware of. I have also personally been temporarily rejected because the court or jail could not find the bail papers; and on another occasion, because the bail order and the jail records did not tally (usually jail records out of date) on the outstanding charges, so that it was not clear that the order covered all charges on which the accused was held. Generally the latter problem occurs when the "outstanding charges" have actually been dismissed or dealt with, so the accused can often clarify it if you can get the Jail and JP to get him there to discuss the difficulty (with follow-up calls to verify his version of the situation).

Another interesting three-step was required by a JP about a year ago during a windstorm in Toronto at the Don Jail. He believed that all sureties had to first see him for initial screening, then go get

Crown approval to do financial screening, and finally come back to him for final decision. Given the timing this required a minimum of a 10-12 hour investment for sureties over a two-day period. My husband with a $40,000 income and $90,000 house and all the earmarks of a professor had to go get Crown approval for a $500 no-deposit bail. The Crown was furious at the parade of minor sureties he was faced with, but was unable to reach the JP in question to discuss it.

I was also personally rejected, along with another surety who had driven 30 miles, because we had been named by the Court but had not gotten a separate letter of Crown approval.

And then there was Mrs. X, a government official. The JP gratuitously informed this very respectable and soft-spoken lady that he would not have accepted her as a surety had not the Crown given approval; the JP also insisted on rewriting the Judge's order, increasing the amount of the surety for her to sign.

Summing up, in the absence of written guidelines available to me as a member of the public, I can only surmise by reactions of Crowns, lawyers, JPs and legislators and representatives of the Attorney General's Office what the proper rules are. But I personally have concluded that *proper guidelines* of Justices of the Peace fall into three categories:

1)   FINANCIAL ADEQUACY FOR THIS BAIL.
Although reasonable in itself and indeed fundamental, this can be and has been abused by demands for specific kinds of property for small bails, bankbooks with specific qualities, knowledge of details of account number and deposit and withdrawal dates by memory, letters from employers, etc.

2)   RELATIONSHIP TO THE ACCUSED.
The surety should have enough of a relationship to the accused, and of the right kind to yield a reasonable likelihood that the accused will appear in court. Again, although important, it is often stretched to the point of arguing that unless a surety can GUARANTEE he can CONTROL the behaviour of the accused, a guarantee no one can make, he is unsuitable. Another obscure area here is how far the surety should be able to "guarantee" the accused will observe other bail conditions: observe 10 p.m. curfews, abstain altogether from drinking, avoid certain places or persons, etc.

3) CRIMINAL RECORD OF SURETY.

It seems reasonable that the surety should be a person of sufficiently good standing in the community to be sure he will not be condoning and encouraging criminal behaviour. As before, the guidelines are obscure and the existence of very minor charges long past are sometimes invoked, while other JPs show wide tolerance to accept sureties with fairly recent, fairly major convictions, but whose current character seems acceptable.

An important factor to note is that the JP interview is entirely openended, so that any of these areas may simply NOT BE COVERED AT ALL in an interview. I have been interviewed as a surety when financial matters have scarcely been considered, and am seldom asked about my possible criminal record, no doubt because of my respectable air. Also some JPs have asked no questions about the depth of my relationship to the accused. A more standard approach might yield more consistent results.

To sum up some of the more dubious turndowns I have known sureties rejected for:

1) Inability to show in cash the full no-deposit bail.

2) Inability to prove they could control accused.

3) Three months not long enough to know accused.

4) Having bailed one or more others. (This one is frequent, still continues, despite flat statement by Attorney General Representative in Hansard record that it is improper.)

5) Bail reduction hearing was pending, though surety willing to sign for full current bail.

6) Only mother could control accused, in view of the JP.

7) Parents with two sons in jail could only collectively bail one of them.

8) Although not actually rejected, strong implication on several occasions that a jail volunteer was immoral to engage in bailing anyone.

9) Excessively stringent judgements on financial ability of surety.

10) Lack of a bankbook to show with exact amount of bail in it.

11) Lack of letter from employer stating length of employment of surety(!)

12) Lack of bankbook, as opposed to bank statement showing current balance beyond amount of surety demanded.

13) Having made a plan for accused, when court had other requirements, despite willingness to accept court requirements when told of them.

14) Various refusals where reasons for rejection were totally unclear and were unstated. ("I don't have to tell you why." as one JP stated to me boldly during his refusal.)

15) Absence of Crown approval even on very small bails, and even in one case where sureties were named in bail order by Judge, at hearing with, of course, the Crown fully represented.

16) At least two instances where JP chose to reject surety knowing surety was Crown approved and had letter.

17) Lack of property (as opposed to other economic resources).

18) JP believed that accused "Doesn't deserve to be out on street.

19) Bail order unclear or papers lost in the system.

20) Very old and minor criminal record.

The above briefly summed up chaos is not a rule of law or of justice, but a kind of combination of anarchy and blind authority, the authority being put in the hands of minor officials with inadequate training to begin to cope consistently with such blanket powers. Until we have CLEAR GUIDELINES PUBLICLY AVAILABLE, SOMETHING IN WRITING GIVEN REJECTED SURETIES, and A CLEAR SYSTEM FOR APPEAL, the system of surety-approval by JPs will continue to function far below the minimum standards needed by a democratic society based on justice and law.

Other Recommendations on Remand Issues:

A)   DUTY COUNSEL available to sureties being estreated in estreatment court. I have sat through 3 days of estreatment court and seen up to 100 cases dealt with each day in about 4 hours. Fewer than 5% of sureties I saw had any counsel, and very few understood the ground of defence in estreatment. Although the Judges were trying to be fair, they were also trying to get through a huge number of cases very quickly. The level of justice, although certainly superior to the JP charades just described, left something to be desired.

B)   CLOSER COOPERATION between Attorney General's Office and Minister of Corrections on many matters which should be joint concerns. *Joint planning and funding on bail programs* and bail hostels to insure professional quality services would be a giant step toward closer cooperation.

C)   BETTER COMMUNICATION with Attorney General's area and rest of justice system. I am sorry if it is tactless to say so, but whether I am talking with the private sector or with persons in a variety of government departments, I am amazed by the unanimity of agreement that it is very difficult to get response and movement from this office. This includes persons working broadly for the Attorney General's Department. I am still waiting to hear from the Attorney General's Office in regard to my recommendations on JPs made a year ago in February. I was told they would be back to me last fall, nearly a year ago.

D)   A SPEEDY TRIAL ACT, such as some American jurisdictions have, would facilitate in many ways the remand situation. For those who do stay in jail, the waiting time is vastly cut. For those who are out, the costs and risks of community supervision are diminished. Justice is also better served when the principals can actively recall the events. We notice a big impact on our caseload in College Park and East Mall. Judge Rice in College Park and Judge Roebuck in East Mall have each instituted systems which gets trials over with within a three month maximum.

E)   THAT YOU INTERVIEW SOME ACCUSED PERSONS who have recently been through the remand experience, for their recommendations. I learned from a very articulate person who happened to be arrested that prisoners in the OCH bullpens are not provided with any free breakfasts, for instance.

F)   That there be CONSULTATIONS ON TIMING OF BAIL HEARINGS between all those attempting to facilitate the bail process, including bail projects which do the verification. In some jurisdictions, afternoon hearings would make a lot of sense, for instance.

G)   That there be clearly stated POLICY ON ACCESS TO REMAND PRISONERS to facilitate those working on bail problems in the initial arrest period. We had to struggle 10 months to get court cell access, and some other areas still have problems in proper access to newly arrested persons in order to do verification and assess for supervision.

H)   REMINDER CLERK: That you consider whether it would add to efficiency enough to justify the cost to appoint a sort of "reminder clerk" whose job would consist of contacting all persons coming up for trial in the last 24-48 hours before, in order to remind them of the time and location. The majority of failures to appear in our experience are carelessness, confusion, or ineptitude; it is possible that such a position would justify itself in terms of court time and costs saved on FTAs. We do this sort of thing, of course, for our own supervision caseload.

I)   That the concept of the PRESUMPTION OF INNOCENCE be made the ground of our policy on remands. The notion that is is ok for people to serve time before trial, and then be given time served when they finally come up, is one I have heard from more than one Judge. Treatment of accused persons during the remand period is at the heart of our whole justice system.

J)   BAIL CONDITIONS: Related to the preceding point, that some examination be given to the kind of bail conditions sometimes laid down. Many are unenforceable, and others are dubious given the presumption of innocence, or irrelevant. I know one instance where a person with no record and charged with fraud had as a bail condition to have no contact with his wife, simply because his mother-in-law came to a bail hearing and badmouthed him. Can there not be a guideline to Judges that bail conditions must at least relate to the criminal record and current charge of the accused?

K)   That the Minister of Correctional Services and the Attorney General jointly establish the ground rules for a system of BAIL HOSTELS where needed. In Toronto, bail hostels would enable us to provide a suitable alternative for many rootless youth, and to diminish FTAs and hopefully new offences charged for persons on bail supervision. About 50% of the cases we get at Old City Hall on bail supervision have no address other than one of the hostels. Existing hostels are not only overly in demand, but are not set up to deal with our clientele.

*   *   *   *   *

This presentation was greeted with hostility by the Commission. The Attorney General's Representative in particular regarded my criticisms of his "Professional JPs" as amateurish, undocumented, picking on exceptions, and wholly unwarranted. The group was unwilling to look at the points in anything but a negative light.

I have taken considerable space in a volume on prison abolition on a specific relatively small point which addresses not so much how prisoners are treated as how their relatives and friends are treated. But I think it highly relevant for it shows not only how far the punitive taint extends, but also how unwilling the justice system is to respond at all to the most determinedly optimistic, positive, and persistent efforts toward change by persons of good will. I think the history here illustrates how carefully and in general, how charitably, I tried to change this part of the system by working through accepted channels. The intransigence of this one part is a part of the intransigence of the whole. When abuses cannot be changed, it is an indication of the need for a whole new approach. The walls between JPs and sureties too, have got to come down.

2.
STORIES OF INDIVIDUAL PRISONERS

I have selected just two stories for this section, from the many we encountered. We went on relating to both these men for some time, and in fact, Steve's family have been very loyal friends to me through many hard times in my own life, and Steve is now out of prison and doing well, in spite of all described in this paper. The question is, why do men have to triumph over all the destructive effects of prison of their lives?

TERRY
LETTER TO THE JUDGE ON BAIL HEARING

Your Honour,

I realize your decision is arrived at by fact and suggestion by both the Crown Attorney and my lawyer and what statements are made in court by myself, but unfortunately I find it impossible to say anything once I'm in court as I feel very self-conscious and usually just remain silent. What I have to say is very very important to my entire future, so I felt that this was the only way to express myself.

I know things do not look their best in regards to my past record. In 1973 I was charged with fraud, cheques were written to the Dominion Stores for food. I was 16 years old at the time and very frightened of going to jail. I was released and I ran off because of my fright. Therefore, a charge of failure to appear was entered against me. I pleaded guilty to those charges and was sentenced to 9 months (definite) and 6 months (indefinite).

In 1975, approximately December, I was charged with accommodation fraud. My wife and I stayed at the Holiday Inn in Oakville for approximately 2 days and I was worried by the information that several guys were coming down with baseball bats looking for trouble, so I left, hoping to miss them. I was unable to make a payment on my car and one of those fellows had co-signed, so I had good reason to believe the information true. I had not received my cheque from work yet, so I was unable to check out, so I left with every intention of returning to pay the $90 bill, but I was charged before I had the chance. I pleaded guilty to the charge and I was sentenced to 2 years probation.

While I was serving my sentence in the Brampton Adult Training Centre, I was given a T.A.P. Their T.A.P. Programme was involving 6 inmates (students). I was one of the students out of the six, two of us completed the programme successfully, myself and another inmate. I was released with a promise to appear when I was charged with Accommodation Fraud and I always appeared in court without hesitation. I knew I could be going to jail, and yet I also knew that failing to appear would only make things much worse as I knew that no matter where I went or what I did I would be caught sooner or later. I believe I appeared in court in excess of 5-8 times.

I appeared in the Oakville Court on the 27th of July, 1976, with Justice of the Peace, M. Allen requesting bail but was refused for three reasons: 1) no address; 2) no one for bail; 3) my failure to appear in 1973. I have been offered temporary residence and the posting of surety bail. This has been offered to me through the untouchable kindness of the Quakers. They are being very generous in their offer, as I well realize, and they know that I'm not trying to prolong justice by getting bail, nor just for the sake of being released until the trial, but for the sake of my marriage. I am married with a little girl aged 7 months, born to us in Mississauga, Ontario.

When I was arrested, many things were left at loose ends between my wife and I. Because of circumstances involved, we lost everything we ever owned. She is presently staying with friends in Mississauga but cannot remain there much longer as they are expecting relatives of theirs to come and stay over for a fair length of time; there would not be enough room for everyone. Thus, leaving my wife to find furniture, clothes, apartment, dishes, and every other conceivable necessity all by herself. She must look after Stacey and she must manage to do all this on $286 a month, which welfare gives her. It is these things that will tear our marriage apart and that I just couldn't bear. Jan and Stacey are the only things in the world that have any real meaning to me. They are my life and with them out of my life, I really would have no life to live.

I know my wrongs and I must pay my debts to society, and I am not challenging that, but the future of my entire life rests with your decision. I am not trying to justify what I have done, now or in the past. I am only asking that you allow me to right my wrongs the best

I can and save the only two things that have any meaning to me. It took putting me in custody and being away from my family to realize how much I love them and what a fool I've been. I can only pray that you allow me to keep what is so dear to me.

I have the low (formal) education of grade eight, I have a criminal record, I am 19 years old (born December 15, 1956), and approximately $10,000 in debt due to a swindler whose 'cons' made him several dollars richer and my credit and financial status at a very poor level. Being in custody has allowed me to stop and realize many things and I have come to the conclusion that these four things were and are at the root of my problems. I can do nothing about my criminal record, except stay out of trouble and eventually request a pardon, my age will naturally change with time. I am making arrangements to declare personal bankruptcy so that my family and I can start fresh and do things right and cautiously this time. I intend to go to university as a mature student, working part time and attend their four year medical course. My eventual goal is to become an M.D. (G.P.).

I now have the chance to change my life before I destroy it and all the decisions I have made to change my life have all been for two reasons...my wife, Janice, and our little girl, Stacey. I want more than anything else in the world to get on the right track and give my family a good, honest life and I believe that these decisions I have made are a step in the right direction, but if I am not given bail, I am sure that my marriage will turn to ashes, as will my dreams and my very life. I only wish I could find the right words to express how I feel. I will agree to any stipulations you impose upon me and I will stick to them without fail. All I ask is that you allow me to straighten everything out with my family, get an apartment, furniture, and clothes for them.

I realize that it must be difficult for you to know how I really feel, and I pray to God that you will know that what I have said is very truthful and that I mean every word.

Thank you,
Terry

BAIL HEARING FOR TERRY

The arrangement we worked out for Terry was that Bert and Irmegard King would give bail for him, and Bert would testify for him at his bail hearing, while our family would offer housing and an ongoing relationship. We wrote a strong letter of support stating all this, and Bert attended the bail hearing. My account of the bail hearing in this case is thus, second-hand.

Briefly, the Judge was at first impressed by the Quaker involvement and paid the usual tributes to Quakers and their work past and present. But the Crown eventually convinced him that Terry was a compulsive chequewriter whose offences would not be stopped by the kinds of support we were offering, and was therefore, too dangerous to be out even temporarily on bail. The crucial evidence was that Terry had written two cheques for cars in a fairly short period – you can only drive one car, therefore, the second cheque was a compulsive desire to show off. Terry's lawyer failed to correct this, although he had explained it to his lawyer. The first of the cars was an ancient one where Terry had been as much swindled as swindler, and which had fallen apart and been junked within two weeks of purchase. Hence, writing a second bad cheque for a car soon afterwards, while reprehensible, was not INCOMPREHENSIBLE, and certainly not compulsive.

The hearing was held in the Judge's Chambers, a more informal setting, and Terry's wife and baby, as well as Bert and the lawyer and the Crown Attorney were present, plus guards with Terry. When the Judge been giving his verdict, denying his bail, Terry and Jan both began to cry. The Judge hurried through his words and rushed out of the room, not wishing to stay and see the consequences of his verdict.

Someone in an attempt at mercy permitted Terry and his wife to embrace briefly, and let Terry try to hold the baby for a moment. Both were awkward operations because he was handcuffed. He was then led away, and Jan was not permitted to ride back to the jail with the guards. Bert offered to bring her to the jail so the two of them could try to piece together some new hopes and plans for the future, or consolation for the present grief. Bert dropped Jan and the baby at the jail, knowing she had arranged for a ride to pick her up from there later in the day.

Fortunately, Bert circled the block, because as he came by again, he found Jan walking down the road carrying the baby, upset and with nowhere immediately to go. Visiting hour was just over, and rules are not broken for the Terrys and Jans of this world. Bert picked her up, talked things over briefly, and arranged to take her to the home where she was staying. He tried to reassure her of our continuing desire to help the family, but it was a bitter ending to a bitter day for all of us.

Bert and Irmegard had to be away the next couple of days, so I phoned Jan the following day, a Saturday, and asked if I could give her a lift out to the jail to visit Terry. She greeted the proposal like our kids do a trip to an amusement park.

Jan, who is only 17 herself, had dressed Stacey, the 7-month-old baby, in a fresh, dainty pink and white outfit, to see her Daddy. We arranged that if the guards would permit it, I would be in for part of the visit, but not all. There were some things I felt the need to clear with Terry myself - a possible change of lawyer for him, and just my face-to-face assurance of firm support. But I was anxious to give them what semblance of privacy a jail permits, by absenting myself from part of the visit. Fortunately the guards we dealt with that afternoon were humane, and it was agreed I could be in for 15 minutes, then call for a guard and take the baby with me, leaving Terry and Jan to visit through the plate glass and wire on their own for the last 15 minutes.

As soon as we had sat down, Stacey began playing games through the glass with her Daddy - rubbing noses across opposite sides of it, patting hands, making faces at each other. I had always hated the isolation and exclusiveness of the glass in that visiting room, but Stacey and Terry transformed it for me into a poignant, but beautiful thing.

After I had taken Stacey out to the park across the street, and was sitting there with her while Terry and Jan had their short visit "through a glass darkly," one of my favourite New Testament verses kept running through my head:

"For I am persuaded that neither death nor life, nor angels, nor principalities, nor heights, nor depths, nor power, nor things present, nor things to come, nor anything else in all creation, will be able to separate us from the love of God in Christ Jesus our Lord." How to make that assurance of unfailing love a reality for Terry and Jan? I know no other way than to do our best to be channels of that love and hope in the very unloving world of jails and courts.

Epilogue

We have been fortunate in finding an excellent lawyer who will take Terry's case, and are now working hard on plans for an early trial and a strong appeal for probation, with the supports we are offering Terry and Jan. Our deepened support appears to have offset the damage of the bail denial, and in his latest letter to us, Terry writes:

"I was becoming very cold again as I did the last time I was in jail, but reading your letter brought warmth, and kindness, and a lot of love back to my heart again. You have made me feel as if I have, after searching all my life, found out not only what I was searching for, but I feel the "cavity" that I've had in my heart and mind, since I can remember, has finally disappeared. I almost feel "light." You know, I think that was all I ever needed, because once I got your letter, it seemed as though, all of a sudden, my problems were solved, I felt stronger, reassured, and most of all, human.

"I feel I know what I want, where I'm going, and how to get there; it all seems so clear. That verse you shared with me has also restored hope and faith to me, as I honestly felt completely shattered. Without you and the other Quakers I would have given up hope entirely, and that "cavity" would still be haunting my soul for years to come. Here I sit, now wanting to help others and try to lighten their burdens. I feel kindness surge within and love for my family and friends. For the first time I feel real sorrow for my deeds. There exists a drive within, that demands that I be me, the way I want to be – to right my wrongs, to be a good father, and give my family a good, clean, honest life. Many would say this is a fool's dream, and if so, then I am a fool's fool, for THIS WILL BE MY REALITY.

"I hope you can see through my outer shell and know how I feel inside. I have never been so open with anyone before."

Here is a man too dangerous to be out on bail!

PAIR WHO WOUNDED OFFICER IN HOLD-UP GET 10, 12 YEARS
TORONTO STAR, Thursday, June 21, 1979

Two men responsible for an armed robbery in which a Metro police officer was slightly wounded have been sentenced to 10 and 12 year penitentiary terms.

"There's no open season on police officers," Chief Justice Gregory Evans of the Supreme Court of Ontario said shortly before passing sentence.

Evans jailed Michael Skraban, 24 of the Westway, for 12 years and Stephen Tucic, 26, of Jane Street, for 10 years. Skraban had a previous record for armed robbery.

In such crimes as robbery, Evans said, "the stakes are high. When you lose you must be prepared to pay the price."

Court was told that on December 28, 1977 the two accused men acquired several stolen weapons. On December 30 they went to the

Red and White supermarket in Etobicoke's Martingrove Plaza near Dixon Road and Highway 401.

Tucic went into the store and Skraban remained outside.

Sgt. Daniel Dukoff and his partner, policewoman, Joyce McKnight, were on routine patrol in the area and Skraban noticed them.

Armed with the sawed-off shotgun, Skraban ordered them out of the police car. The officers got out, but Dukoff grabbed at Skrab's weapon and tried to disarm him.

The gun discharged and three pellets struck Dukoff in the leg.

Skraban also fired at the police car. During the struggle, Skraban shot himself in the finger before fleeing the scene.

Dukoff then went into the store and ordered Tucic to drop his cut-down rifle. Tucic started to swing his gun around at Dukoff and the officer fired his service revolver. The bullet struck Tucic in the jaw.

He was arrested in the basement of the store and Skraban was arrested four days later in a Kipling Avenue house.

The two accused apologized for their behaviour but Evans said that "it is only poor shooting rather than lack of intent" that resulted in the officer suffering just a slight wound.

Skraban "intended to 'wipe out' a police officer," the Judge added.

He said the police officers "should be commended for their restraint in a situation which was highly dangerous and involved risks to them."

STEVE TUCIC - June, 1979

Reading this article from the *Toronto Star*, one would get the impression that all is well in the world again. Two dangerous robbers have been apprehended, justice has been served, the police have performed even more heroically than usual, and the world is a safer place for the events described. The two criminals will be sent away for many years to a place where they will be both punished and reformed at the same time—wonder of wonders. Our continued faith in the efficacy of prisons to do two contradictory things at once in the face of their 85% failure rate is matched only by our impressive faith in the theory of deterrence. Our faith in deterrence is undeterred by this 85% return rate for those who go all through our court and prison system, or by our continued high crime rate, despite a very high rate of imprisonment in Canada.

CRUMBLING WALLS: WHY PRISONS FAIL

The article in *the Star* is not bad reporting. It states fairly objectively what went on in court, with better accuracy and less hysteria and editorializing than many. Which goes to show how often there is more to a story than meets the eye, and that behind every such brief piece in the papers are human stories involving deep tragedy, farce, or comedy. I was in the court the day, I know Steve Tucic, and I think it may be helpful to look at some of the truths behind the truth.

Where do armed robbers come from, what kind of people are they, and where do they go?

I met Steve last November in Toronto West Detention Centre, as part of my visiting program there. One of the things the article didn't mention was that Steve and his co-accused spent 18 months in maximum security jail custody before they ever came to trial. Even then, they got the trial because they finally pleaded guilty, nor did they demand a jury trial. A jury trial is a great luxury if you are in custody, because it delays still further your trial date.

If they did it, you may ask, why didn't they plead guilty straight away instead of waiting so long? Because the Crown wanted them to plead guilty to attempted murder, which neither of them felt guilty of, and until he was willing to drop this charge, no agreement could be reached. This kind of bargaining process with the pressure of months of waiting in incarceration is a frequent part of the legal process.

The 18 months they waited will not count out of sentenced time – it is what is called "dead time." It is time taken out of the life of an accused person, and never compensated for. If he is acquitted, there are rarely apologies for dead time, certainly no direct compensation. If he is convicted, the Judge supposedly takes it into account in sentencing. But as in this case, there is often little indication that he has done so, since these sentences are already well above average for armed robbery. Dead time is considered extra tough: you have the anxiety of waiting for trial, you don't know for sure when it will come or what will happen, and you are incarcerated in a jail with few recreational or educational programs or opportunities. It is considered so onerous some Judges have stated as a rule of thumb that it should count 2 to 1 for time served after sentencing.

Yet neither when Steve and Michael pleaded guilty, nor at their sentencing was any regret expressed by Crown or Judge for the incredibly long delay and dead time served. Many American jurisdictions simply count dead time out after sentence is given, thus making it no longer dead time.

Steve first came to me for help for his younger brother. His reaction about his own life was summed up to begin with: "I've made a mess of things for myself, and there is probably not very much you could do for me. I am looking at at least 5 years probably. But Danny is young and wasn't involved, and I'd appreciate it if you can help him." So I began by looking into Danny's situation, but I continued to visit Steve.

He appreciated my interest, and we began to talk about Steve's own situation. The one thing he wanted most of all was a chance for treatment. He recognized that he had problems, and he wanted help with them. He had had a psychiatric report which stated that he was dangerous and prone to violence. He was incensed about this, but in a quiet, mannerly way. He argued rationally, "If I'm so violent, why didn't I ever even raise my gun when I was shot by a policeman in this robbery?" But he made no pretence that he had not done the armed robbery, or that it was in any way justifiable as an action. He had done something both wrong and stupid, and he would have to meet the consequences. But the one thing he hoped to get was treatment so that he could conquer the problem in him that had led to this behaviour. It seemed a hope which was neither unreasonable nor incompatible with the goals of society for its own safety.

Meanwhile Steve did his best with the situation he was in. He was involved in some of the education, chapel, and art programs in the institution, about all there was going, as well as getting counselling-visits with me. All this was a small fraction of the time, most of which was sitting and waiting, but it was the best he could manage. He was involved in the efforts of a few others to start a jail newspaper, and contributed both poems and articles to it. He read and thought a good deal about different systems for dealing with crime, and we talked about what did and did not make sense, what were some of the changes most needed, and why.

At Christmas, Steve was looking forward to a simple chapel Christmas party. Parties are limited inside a prison – so many things we take for granted are contraband and forbidden. Still it was the first event of any significance to look forward to in nearly a year inside. Then someone said Steve had to go to the Don Jail for a remand at that time. A remand is a routine appearance in court to state that you are still in custody and will appear next on such and such a date to have the same thing said, with no date necessarily in mind for a real hearing.

Missing the Christmas party for a routine remand would have been frustrating, but Steve and others were convinced they had no remand at that time, and that it was a clerical error. However, the institution personal declined to check, and they were shipped, despite their protests, to the Don, just missing the event they had hoped to be a part of. Sure enough, there was no remand, just a clerical error...

I continued to visit Steve every week or two. His stay inside seemed perpetual to me as well as to him by now. We talked about different things, details of imprisonment, occasional news of his family, what had been happening at the jail and in my life. Steve was neither so bitter about his situation nor so casual about his offences as some I talked with.

One day, we talked about his last time in prison for an offence, in 1972-73. This was in response to an offence Steve was alleged to have participated in for breaking and entering to steal. A police officer maintained he had hidden in the trunk of a car, overheard Steve confessing to the crime, and written down in neat, straight lines in his notebook an account of the conversation. The defence brought in two expert witnesses to testify that it was impossible in the dark to write straight lines as legibly and neatly as those in the notebook, but nonetheless, Steve was convicted.

It was the only offence he had ever been convicted of wherein he stoutly maintained his innocence. His mother and others also believed that the policeman had deliberately framed him. It was one of those cases one hears of where a policeman has taken a dislike, often understandable to begin with, to a young man; then pursues and hounds him to the point where he is harassed even in situations when he is doing his best to follow the letter of the law. Not only was Steve convicted, but he got a heavy sentence of three years for the incident, though he only served 5 months before he was freed on an appeal. In the course of appeals, Steve got discouraged and left for the U.S., though he should have stayed in Canada to see the matter through. He built a good record in the U.S., working steadily about 4 years before his past caught up with him and he was deported back to Canada for his record.

Steve was neither overly inclined to talk about his past, nor exceptionally reticent when we got into it. So details of his history came out from time to time as something brought them up. Steve had had the bad luck at 17 to get a "heavy" Judge for his first offences, a few "break and enters." The general practice with first offences of a nonviolent sort by a young person is to try probation, but Steve instead got sentenced to 6 months definite, 5 months indefinite, 6 months concurrent, and 2 years probation. He went to

Guelph, and had it not been for the recent riot in Guelph, I might have never learned more about his experiences as a 17-year-old there.

On the day when the papers were featuring the execrable conditions of the inmates put into the lightless tunnel in Guelph after the recent riot there, I mentioned the subject to Steve. To my surprise, he responded, "Yes, I know what it is like. I was there in '70, during my first time in prison." The implication from reading the papers was that it was a once-and-only horror show, to meet the shocking destruction of $37,000 worth of government property by the inmates.

The papers later boasted that the institution was getting the whole $37,000 back from inmates' small pay and allowances to recover the damage. It also boasted that inmates had been saddled with years of extra time. I computed the cost to the taxpayer of the extra time listed in the paper, and found we will be paying ABOUT A THIRD OF A MILLION DOLLARS in added cost to keep inmates in this extra time. Yet the papers made no mention of the really major financial cost of the riot, only of the property damage.

I asked Steve more about his experience after the Guelph riot of his day. All inmates on the offending units, regardless of guilt or innocence, were totally stripped. They were put naked into the tunnel, without any proper light, adequate food, or sanitary facilities. Homosexuals began celebrating in one corner in their way, while the rest were left to make of the situation what they could. They were threatened with tear gas and hoses if there were any complaining.

Stripped of all human dignity, without right of trial or defence, they were punished in this way for days. But already by 17, Steven had learned how small his rights were. He explained to me that he took it for granted that whatever happened had to be-he didn't question it at the time. What has happened already to a 17-year-old boy who can experience such degradation and know he has no right to complain, only to be further scarred.

Steve also explained to me that he knew a part of his problem related to his father, who had beaten him when Steve was little. But he didn't belabour the topic, or blame his father or society for where he was now. Only he knew it was part of dealing with his problem to understand some of the roots of it, so he referred to it from time to time.

Finally, his trial date drew near, and Steve asked me for help in two ways. First, he wanted to find the section of the Parliamentary Commission on Penitentiaries Report which protests the lack of adequate treatment for inmates in federal institutions. Secondly, he asked me if I would be present at his hearing, partly to see what happened, but also to be with his mother. The last time he was sentenced – the time they both agreed he had done nothing – she had fainted in court when he was sentenced. This time he would get much heavier time, and he didn't want her to be there alone.

I found the Report for him, and his lawyer referred to it in his brief. And I came to court, and sat next to his mother. Things got off to a bad start as the Don Jail failed to send Michael Skraban, Steve's co-accused, to court. Court adjourned till 11:15 to give them time to get him there. When we finally began again, the defence attorneys made their pleas. The Judge interrupted both defence lawyers fairly regularly with comments, mostly derogatory of the defendants. He was not so extreme in this as some Judges I've seen, but court hearings often give the feeling of an older brother trying to intercede with a stern father for an erring younger sibling. The older brother has not disgraced himself, but is in a disadvantageous position, and the authority and wrath of Papa will descend on him if Papa feels his defence of the younger brother tries to justify his conduct.

One point which both defence attorneys argued with the Judge was whether the fact that the policeman wounded was by common consent so slightly wounded he hadn't even needed a band-aid, should in any way alleviate the criminals' sentence. The courts clearly recognize that murder is a worse offence than attempted murder, although the offender is often just lucky it was not murder. Similarly, when a victim has suffered serious and/or permanent injuries, the offence is treated more seriously than if the injury is slight and passing. This is both logical and illogical as we can see, but it is paradoxical that although everyone rightly condemns a defendant where there is a serious injury, there is a reluctance to admit that his situation should be any better when there is not.

Among the other point that disturbed me in the hearing were:

1. CONGRATULATING POLICE FOR THEIR RESTRAINT IN USE OF FIREARMS

The Judge congratulated the police for their restraint in the use of firearms in this case, although Steve was shot in the face when he never came close to using his gun. One of the points Steve made later in discussing the hearing with me is that in order to get the Crown to drop the attempted murder charge, they had to agree to let the Crown present its version of the facts and the defence swallow them. This was so painful that I could see each defendant at various points shaking their head at things they legally accepted as going on the record. This kind of quid pro quo from the bargaining process is frequent, and results in a statement of facts which is an AVERAGE of STRENGTH of two contending forces, rather than the closest thing to truth the two can arrive at.

One of the significant "facts" stated in the Crown's statement was that Steve pointed the rifle at one point. He insists that this was not so, that he didn't even know how to use it, a fact no one brought out. He did not hear the policeman call to surrender. As to his not surrendering after he was shot, he ran, he felt, to save his life. When he was down in the basement, bleeding heavily, he heard the policeman shout, "I'm gonna kill you, you bastard." Any one working long in the system knows the widespread concern about the extent of police violence both in the station house and outside. Steve faked being unconscious and felt it saved his life. Yet he was blamed by the Judge for not surrendering. How could a Judge, predisposed as they are to believe the police speak only truth and defendants when they differ only falsehood, be expected to believe such a statement, even had court procedure permitted Steve to express his version of what happened?

Whatever the facts, shooting a man who admittedly never pulled a trigger in the face is not in my opinion an extent of restraint which deserves special judicial commendation.

2. CROWN'S ROLE IN DETERMINING SENTENCE

The general public does not usually realize how much the final sentence of a convicted person is a bargaining process, influenced by a strange mixture of factors: how strong the Crown's case is, how many charges are laid, length of defendant's record, amount of community support defendant has, effectiveness of defence lawyer, amount of time Crown is prepared to put on it, and disposition of Judge. Some Judges are notoriously hard or soft.

One of the rules of the system carried down through numerous precedents is that a person who pleads guilty, thereby saving the taxpayer thousands of dollars for a costly and often long trial, gets a lighter sentence than one who pleads innocent but is eventually convicted. This rule in itself has some questionable results–the truly innocent are more likely to plead innocent, so if convicted wrongly, they often get longer sentences than the guilty. Nonetheless, it is standard practice, one of the many "incentives" to oil the wheels of the system and keep it moving toward convictions and prisons.

In this case, the Crown asked for life sentences for both these young men, 24 and 26, despite the fact that:

1) One of them, Steve, had no prior offence of a violent type.

2) No one but themselves was at all seriously injured during the offence.

3) There is no case in Canadian jurisprudence of life being given for armed robbery.

4) They had pleaded guilty, saving a full trial.

5) The Crown had promised Steve's lawyer to ask no more than 10 years if he would plead guilty.

I don't know why the Crown took such an extreme measure, but I heard two explanations from various people. One was that Michael Skraban had been arrested previously for a robbery on which he was acquitted, but the police were convinced he was guilty. Now that they had him on another charge, the hope was to make up in sentence for what he had got by with (in their opinion) before.

Whether this was true in this instance, I don't know, but this kind of thinking – trying to equalize the justice balance in a system which is bound at best to be fraught with inequalities – is the same kind of thinking that leads some police to beat up accused persons when arrested, to be sure they get SOME punishment for their misdeeds. It is also the same kind that leads defendants when they serve time and suffer all the injustices of the court and prison system to feel *they* have to equalize the scales by going out to commit more crimes to right the balance. In short, the courts really satisfy almost no one, and most of those involved try to right the balance of justice behind the scenes in ways destructive to society.

The other explanation was that this Crown was trying to acquire a reputation as a tough Crown who got a lot of time. Such an ambition is understandable in our status-conscious society. But when success means sending people away for more years to an institution which is at least 85% certain to return them more dangerous and bitter, it would be an excellent practice to require that Crowns have some experience of what a prison is like.

The Crown also argued that they should be put away for the protection of society, and were too dangerous to be allowed out. Yet there is a specific legal provision for doing this, which he did not use. As one defence lawyer said, don't try to get a long sentence on such a ground, instead of using the law provided for this; the problem being, he knew they would not fit this law – another case of trying to equalize things in ways outside the law.

3.   PSYCHIATRIC REPORTS

Many prisoners I have worked with are very suspicious of psychiatry and psychiatrists. No wonder, when one sees the use they are put to in courts. Their testimony is pounced on by either side to support their own views, and frequently the main point is distorted. Their reports are often used as reasons to send men for many years to institutions which will only destroy them; which makes one wonder about the morals of lending themselves to the process at all.

Two psychiatric reports on Steve were used, both of which spoke of his need and desire for treatment, and recommended it. But they also contained some negative evaluations, and one spoke of him as dangerous and potentially violent. This was used heavily by the Crown in asking for the life sentence. I sometimes wonder how many of us could be sure no psychiatrist would label us potentially violent. One study of guards and inmates in prison found little difference in this dimension, if anything the guards coming out with a higher violence profile.

Yet these reports are frequently based on relatively short contact under stressful conditions, when the men know they are being weighed up in ways that will influence their whole future. Prison chaplains who have seen them day to day in relatively relaxed conditions are rarely asked for their opinions. The myth of the magic of psychiatric training making one infallible prevails to a great extent in court, and ironically makes most prisoners suspicious of the profession.

Although both psychiatric reports recommended treatment for Steve, and although the plea for treatment was at the root of both his lawyer's and his statements, the Judge in sentencing at first MADE NO RECOMMENDATION FOR TREATMENT. Even after his lawyer repeated the plea, the Judge muttered that he thought it best left to the wisdom of system, which showed again how little he knew the system he was putting these men into.

Although a Judge's recommendation for treatment is no guarantee a man will get it, it's a great help, and he is fighting an uphill sruggle to obtain it without, as I have found in a number of cases. The Judge did finally, reluctantly add a sentence suggesting treatment "if necessary."

4. LEARNING FROM IMPRISONMENT – PRISON AS AN "OPPORTUNITY"

Probably the thing that upset me most of all was this concept, which came through from the Judge repeatedly: that prison was an opportunity to learn. He challenged Skraban during Skraban's statement of contrition with: "You served time before – why didn't you learn from this opportunity?" What can a defendant say in such a circumstance? It is obvious the Judge has never stepped inside a prison, and has no idea what kind of nonsense he is talking, or what kind of an opportunity he had there. The fact is, he HAD learned from this imprisonment exactly what it is best designed to teach. That was why he was here, facing a charge of armed robbery.

Skraban answered the Judge with something insincere and equally foolish about being young and immature. With the Judge holding over his head a life sentence, how could he argue with him over his fundamental misconceptions?

After the sentences were passed, while the defendants were still standing helpless before the Judge, he concluded with, "You may not think these are short sentences, but I've been generous to you. Now don't waste this opportunity, because you may not get another one." Opportunity: 12 and 10 years in prison?! No man who knew the system he was sentencing them to could talk in this way. I thought of young Steve Tucic, at 17 being thrust into a dark, foul, unsanitary tunnel, naked and exposed to every humiliation. HE HAD LEARNED. He would learn more. What kind of man would emerge?

Epilogue

I went home with Steve's mother, and her anger and frustration were inevitable. Left to raise 5 children by herself when her husband returned to Europe, she had coped the best she could.

Steve had been a good son. Even after the incident when they agreed he was framed by the persistent police officer, he had come back and made a new life for himself. Now in one fell swoop, his youth and the remains of that effort were gone. Steve and his mother both recognized he had done wrong. But she felt deep bitterness toward the policeman who had hounded him all these years. Ironically, he had died a year ago, leaving 5 children too. She knew if was terribly wrong, but sometimes she couldn't help hoping his wife would have some of the troubles she had had, and would understand what it was to try to raise boys without a father.

This kind of bitter thinking is wrong. Armed robbery is wrong. But are there not some other wrongs in this story? Have we no better answers, no better way for the Steve Tucics? With two psychiatric recommendations for treatment, and an official government report admitting there is no adequate treatment in prison, are we not wrong to speak of ten years in our destructive prisons as an "opportunity?"

Creative alternatives to imprisonment exist, and have been demonstrated more effective than prisons. When through a long prison term we destroy a Steve Tucic who wants help to change now, we are doing more than endangering the public safety by creating through the very courts and prisons designed to "protect," a more dangerous person. We are also saying no to a human spirit, struggling to grow in the Light, just as you and I are.

3.
MINORITIES IN OUR JUSTICE SYSTEM

If in every other way, our justice system made sense, I would still be an abolitionist because of its totally inequitable role in selecting and oppressing minority groups. Courts and prisons ARE racism in living action. American abolitionists are particularly clear on this point. At a 1983 religious conference on the church and prisons, leaders like Carol Bergman and Walter Collins repeatedly pointed out prisons are like a modern form of slavery. It was not a new thought to me: working at Old City Hall in the courts, I often saw black men tightly handcuffed, being led around by white guards, and visions of the old slave ships and the whole slavery history would pass before my eyes.

What Walter Collins, Carol Bergman, Frank Dunbaugh and others have pointed out is this: the prison issue in the U.S. is a race issue. Incarceration rates for U.S. whites are moderate in the western world, but the 10 times higher black incarceration rate accounts entirely for the uniquely high American rate of incarceration!

Collins also pointed out prisons are a class issue, and argued that those in prison are poor people who rebel: "We put people in prison for being poor, and for rebelling against being poor. People are then defined by those 2–5 minutes of their lives that put them in prison; prisons have very limited ability to see anyone as a whole person." Collins also pointed out that prisons are the only institution where the consumer is always wrong, and where the only people who know what is going on have no voice and are not believed. He concluded with the dramatic statement quoted earlier: "Prisons represent our acceptance that some (black poor) people are expendable."

Lest some Canadians take comfort that black/white racism is a problem limited to the U.S., I must report on some research I did in our Toronto courts. The research had to do with the effectiveness of our Bail Program in meeting its goals. I was not studying racism, or looking for its effects. The effects of racism were so blatant, they forced themselves on my attention. I found statistically significant results in our Toronto courts in 1982 in a careful sample study that a black is much more likely to be held in jail while awaiting trial than is a white. You have to have a lot more problems as a white to get detained than you do as a black: whites in detention had more alcohol and drug problems, more convictions, more institutional experience, more failures to appear in court, more failures to comply with court orders, and more involvement with probation and parole.

Sickening as these findings were to me, the impact of them was even more revolting. There wasn't even a shrug. Fearful of the impact on my job, I cautiously released them where I could, only to find no one was the least bit surprised or interested. When I referred to them in a report on our research to the then Deputy Minister of Corrections, Archie Campbell, he responded, "Why are we even listening to these things here? They are no concern of ours." Racism in our courts and prisons is here to stay, and it is known and accepted.

Another form of racism blatant in both the U.S. and Canada is our treatment of Native people. The following article printed in Canadian Dimension in 1985, documents this fully.

3A.
"ONE INDIAN'S AS GOOD AS ANOTHER"
Native People and The Canadian Justice System[1]

A few years ago I asked a friend, "Where is Bill S?" Bill was a
Native friend of ours, and I hadn't seen him for awhile. She laughed
and replied, "Oh, he's serving time for his brother this week."

"What!" I exclaimed, "You can't do that – what do you mean?"

"Oh, that's just the way the Native people are," she explained.
"When they have anything, they share it, and when they don't they
expect others will give. It's a very caring way of life.

In this case, Bill's brother was up for another liquor charge,
and with his record he would certainly get time, but his wife was
expecting a baby. So Bill offered to serve the time for him. Bill went
to court, pled guilty, and is serving time for his brother in jail now."

Honest, that's what she said, and that's what happened.

When I expressed wonder that the justice system didn't check
appearance and fingerprints, and object to this exchange, she said:
"Oh, what do they care. One Indian's the same as any other to them."

The two halves of this story express the saga of Native people
and our justice system. On the one hand, Native people express
such a level of community caring that they will even go to prison for
each other; on the other, a system of justice grinds Indians through
its ravenous jaws so systematically and impersonally that it
doesn't even notice the substitution of one brother for another, so
long as it can digest another Indian.

Native Children:

The dreary picture of white men's ways of dealing with Native
people continues generation after generation. Beginning with children, the figures in Ontario, typical of most of Canada, are:

Native children are twice as likely to be admitted to detention
homes for the first time.
Native children are twice as likely to be placed on probation.
Native children are three and a half times as likely to be
admitted to Children's Aid facilities.
Native children are four times as likely to be committed to
training schools as all other children.
(Indian Children in Ontario's Juvenile Justice and Child
Welfare Systems, 1983–84.)

Our readiness to break up the Indian family goes back many generations. It sows the seed for the high rate of Native alcoholism so widely known and documented. But these figures show that the effects are visible early – in children separated from their families, and in the very high risk of going to children's prisons, politely called training schools.

Adult Natives and Prisons:

Stan Jolly, in a depressingly repetitive fact sheet called *Warehousing Indians,* has documented the extreme overrepresentation of Native people of every age group in prisons. The table below sums up a sordid picture.

Greater Risks of Natives of Different Ages of Going to Prison in Ontario.
1981-82

Age Group	Native Men	Native Women
16-26	3 times as likely	6 times as likely
26-35	4 times as likely	8 times as likely
36-50	5 times as likely	13 times as likely
51-70	6 times as likely	15 times as likely

It is hard to say which is more striking in these figures: the fact that there are considerable differences, with older Native women suffering the greatest relative injustice; or the monotonous sameness of the fact that in all age groups and for both sexes, Native people are far more likely to be fodder for the justice system than others. Jolly states: "For Native people, Ontario's justice system is a colossal failure. It does not deter; nor does it rehabilitate." If it weren't for the fact that Mr. Jolly's organization, like so many Native support groups, is 100% funded by the government, he might have felt freer to observe that the comment about the justice system's colossal failure applies equally well to non-Native prisoners. But even Mr. Jolly's patience is strained, as he concludes with this query: "What is the point of doing meticulous research on issues involving inmates...if nothing changes?..."

RUTH MORRIS

RISK OF INCARCERATION IN ONTARIO
1981 – 1982

Kenora: Who is the Criminal?

Nothing better illustrates the real issue behind the Native "crime rate" than Kenora. Natives in this area make up 25–30% of the population, but 75% of the male jail admissions and 94% of the female jail admissions. Going to jail is virtually reserved for Natives in this area. Why is this so?

If Kenora/Grassy Narrows rings a bell, it is because of the smouldering issue of mercury pollution, which led the government after great pressure to close the waters to sport fishermen, and even to Native consumption of the fish. This step – taken after great political pressure through the NDP, Native support groups, and ecologists–may have slowed down progress of the dreaded Minimata disease from mercury destruction of the nervous system. But it also virtually ended employment for Natives in the area, whose main occupations as guides and supports for sports tourists were effectively finished by white industry's destruction of their waters.

Unemployment in the area for Natives is nearly 100%. In the face of white civilization's destruction of their livelihood, natural habitat, way of life, and serious threat to their health, Native people have responded with an even higher than usual rate of alcoholism. (Many alcohol offences, it should be noted, are not really offences for whites, only for Natives.) Yet, in this situation neither government nor industry was labelled a criminal: no, it is the Natives who are the criminals!

Conclusions:

Another Native person illustrated our double standard when he offered to become an archeologist and dig up white graveyards. Unthinkable! Yet how little we respect Native graveyards. Native religion is only just gaining the right to be practiced by prisoners in Canada, thanks to the efforts of Native spiritual leaders like Art Solomon. But one Native exprisoner I talked to spoke of the ways our prison system jeers at medicine men and those who go to them, unlike their behaviour toward chaplains. We may ask ourselves, "Has anything changed in the 100 years since we killed Louis Riel?" One Native I asked this question of responded with a smile, "They've just modernized things a little, that's all." Having stolen this country from the Native people, having done so much to destroy their culture, having exposed them to intolerable health conditions and the destruction of much of their family life, we solve the resultant problems by jailing them. It is past time for us to end the gross injustice of our incarceration of generations of Native people in our jails

*   *   *   *   *

Increasingly today we are aware of women as an oppressed group, so the question arises, "What about the treatment of women by courts and prisons?" The answer is not so simple as it is for blacks and Natives. On the surface, women appear to be favoured: in every culture, women have a rate of incarceration 1/4 to 1/20 that of men. But beneath the surface favouritism is an ugly record of failure. Women in trouble with the law suffer from the double oppression by a male-dominated justice system, and sex role domination and physical abuse from lower class male prisoners from minority groups themselves. The one person the black or Native prisoner is allowed by our society to oppress, is his woman.

The story below illustrates some of these points. Although Bettina Harris is a very unusual woman – a fighter who does not hesitate to fight physically for survival and what she sees as her rights – nonetheless, her story is typical of the tragedies back of the lives of most women prisoners.

3B
WOMAN IN PRISON[2]

"When you take away everything a person has, you make them desperate. And when you make them desperate, you make them dangerous. They used to say they were protecting society, but they made animals. They conditioned, controlled, and made those girls into revolving door syndromes."

Bettina Harris is 24 years old, tough, bright, eloquent. Bettina has 58 convictions, and has spent 12 years in juvenile, provincial adult, and federal adult institutions. Her story illustrates what it is like to be a minority of minorities: a woman prisoner.

Early Life

Bettina's mother, keen to be up with the times in the 1960s, got involved with a black man in the U.S., a pimp with criminal connections. Pregnant, she fled to Canada, spending the rest of her life feeling guilty toward Bettina for making her black.

One of Bettina's earliest, most recurrent memories was her mother's saying, during suicidal bouts, "I'm really sorry I made you black." Bettina got the message: her blackness was responsible for her mother's repeated suicide attempts.

Bettina's other early memory was of sitting on the step outside her house. Her mother would drink herself into a stupor till 3 or 4 a.m. and constantly try to get Bettina to come in. Bettina didn't run away, but she wouldn't come in to her drunken mother. "I never went anywhere, cause I had nowhere to go ," recalled Bettina, "I'd sit right there on the little sidewalk, and she would scream and holler and beg me to come in, and I would refuse. What I was trying to say, had I had logic and verbalization was, 'I don't want to be there when you are like that. I love you, I don't want the part-time Mommy that leaves me sometimes. I want you always. When you're like this, I don't want to be there.' So I sat out there, and it was a stand."

When Bettina was 11, her mother called in the Children's Aid, and Bettina was declared "unmanageable." It's an interesting aspect of sexism in our society that girls are much more likely than boys to be charged simply with "incorrigibility" - general refusal to submit to family discipline. Children's Aid wasted no time in half measures. Bettina went to no foster homes, nor were efforts made to remedy the home situation.

She was taken straight to a group home. Bettina describes herself at this point as an angry child. "In school, I was good in grades, but I used to fight with boys, girls, anyone. I was fighting because I felt different. My mother felt guilty, passed it on to me, and I passed it on in anger and violence. But I never knew outward violence till the group home."

Group Home Life

"I met a group called the Devil's Angels there. I learned the ropes from the girls the first night: the girls against the staff." Bettina was introduced immediately into the group code of sneaking out into the park, and of gang life.

But she also made two close friends who meant a lot to her: Candy and Michelle. At 11, peers begin to become important to most children. To a child as starved of normal family life as Bettina, and the other girls in the group home, peer friendships become overwhelmingly important.

The only time in our long and trauma-filled interview when Bettina totally broke down was in talking about Michelle. Less than 2 months after Bettina's entry into the group home, she found her friend Michelle in the park, semi-conscious, beaten and gang-raped.

Even now, Bettina blames Children's Aid for not protecting these children from such horrors. When I asked her later in our talk if anyone in her life had ever been truly kind or tried to help, perhaps a social worker, she responded: "Social worker! I was half black in a totally white system. I was from an emotionally disturbed background. My father was a criminal. I didn't have a chance in Hell in that system. They used to say, 'Tsk tsk, she's intelligent, it's a shame.' My intelligence was a liability: they fought me all the way."

Feeling abandoned, the children's gangs had their own way of dealing with such terrible trauma as Michelle's gang-rape.

"My boyfriend Woody promised revenge. That night after Michelle was found, we went down to have a rumble. For the first time I could have killed somebody and had no conscience. The leader of the other gang was called Snake. He grabbed me, and held a knife to my throat. He held me up to our gang as an enticement, because I was Woody's girlfriend.

"The night before, Woody had given me a knife. I didn't want it, but for some reason I had it with me. And suddenly, there I was with Snake's knife at my neck. For Michelle, for myself, I found myself saying, 'There is nobody here. Nobody is going to protect me. I have no parent. This system is not going to protect me, it's going to use me.' So I plunged the knife into his shoulder with pleasure, and if I had the same thing to do over, I would. I actually don't think I did anything wrong, compared to the things that happened to me or to Michelle."

No one reported this incident to the police. Snake recovered, and in fact, went on to be a "Big biker." Bettina went through a period of disassociation from her repeated shocks.

The group home blamed Bettina and her friends for being the wrong type of girls. Had they been the right types, they would not have been there in the first place.

This familiar syndrome of blaming the victim was accentuated by a psychology test Bettina took not long after these incidents. The psychologist found Bettina had images of violence! Of course he didn't know she had found her best friend brutally raped and permanently damaged, or any of the rest. Whereas the system considered all the girls abnormal, the girls accepted the little differences among one another. But this too led to misunderstandings with the more "normal" staff view.

"There was a girl named Trudi who had been molested by her father, so she was freaky scared of men. One time a male staff was going toward Trudi. We told him to stop, but he kept coming. A fight broke out, and I cracked him over the head with a vase. I was charged with threatening and assault, because I threatened to break up the house if he didn't let Trudi alone."

Detention Center

Bettina describes what it is like for a child to enter our Juvenille Dentention Center for the first time: "Trudi had been in 311 Jarvis 13 times; I had never been there. She ended up going home. That place is terrible: I knew it was a jail. I was 11 years old. I remember exactly how I felt when they made you go in this little cell with a toilet, and a steel bed, and the terrible, clanging echo when they shut that steel door behind you, with keys jangling. It looked exactly like the West Detention Center cells (adult women's jail) do today.

"But before that they had deloused me. They check your body in places where at 11 years of age I had never been touched. I had never done more than kiss. This big hairy, masculine type aggressive matron who wasn't sensitive at all did the strip search; she just figured we were bad children, that was that. So I felt pretty degraded. And then that clanging, ringing door. I remember thinking over and over, 'You must really be bad, or you wouldn't be here.' No words could change the opinion, because otherwise I wouldn't be here."

Left alone with these overwhelming feelings, Bettina unravelled a toothpaste tube, and found a razor-sharp edge. She did not want to die, but she wanted to hurt herself. Three days later she came to fully, and found herself on the way to court, arms heavily bandaged. The Judge kept saying, "Tsk, tsk, such a young girl, why would you want to kill yourself?"

She tried to explain her imitation of her mother, but it made no sense to the grownup Judge. With adult court logic, the Judge concluded, "For your protection, and for society's protection, we're going to send you to Training School."

No one in court saw the irony: taking a girl so sensitive that a single day in detention had driven her to cut her wrists, and putting her into a jail-like environment for years to "protect" her! But Bettina saw it. And her greatest virtue and vice both were that she was never quiet about things. She says now reflecting on it, "There was no explaining. I was a child. It was their system. In their eyes, I had no feelings, no logic, and no rights."

But at the time she was led out screaming, "You can send me anywhere, but I'll be damned if I'll accept it."

"I spat in the Judge's face."

Training School

Bettina arrived in Training School a fully committed and experienced rebel.

She was a natural organizer. She quickly began to get across to the girls that with 200 kids, four segregation cells, and relatively few staff at any one time, there was no way they could control the girls. The truce that ensued involved the authorities giving Bettina her own TV, her own radio, special privileges of all kinds – as long as she desisted from organizing.

But confused as Bettina was by now, a part of her could not be bought off. She felt the authorities were manipulating the kids, that the psychologists were destroying what was left of their sense of self-worth. Bettina had her own campaign of trying to tell the girls they were worth something. She would say, "You don't have to take all this – They get $200 a day for you." But she laments that she was too 'screwed up' herself to begin to meet the yawning chasm of need all around her.

When asked about being a woman in the system, Bettina said, "A woman in the system is 10 times, 100 times more devastated, because it's a man's world in and out of the system, and women even in the subculture are demeaned. You're to be used sexually. I broke the code in both cultures."

A Cry From The Dark

Bettina graduated to the adult system, and the rest of her life to date had been a tragic continuation of these beginnings. She sees now that one main purpose of her life is to be a voice of the few survivors from among the young women she grew up with. While in the institutions, she fought the institutional message: "They kept pounding on their heads, 'You are no good; you're worthless; you're useless.' And I would say, 'No, you're not, these guys are fucked up. They don't know what they are talking about.' So I would reverse the mechanism."

When I asked what had happened to the girls she knew in group home and training school, she replied, "About a third are in the adult system; a third are dead; and a third are in mental institutions. There are four women I know who aren't in any of those situations, and three of them only made it because they married some guy that still beats them." She went on to say that the mental institutions let you go every six months, then send you out to return quickly, with the same revolving door syndrome. The deaths were mainly from violence and drugs.

Bettina explained her own violence in this way. "I have a lot of guilty emotions. I didn't want to hurt people. I didn't want to be a very angry person. I hated the things it made me into. But I never hurt people outside. I always fought police. I have 15 assaults on my record: all of them are police and security guards. Their use of unnecessary and illegal violence towards me and others makes it acceptable for me to be violent to them. I could not justify myself otherwise. Bettina has to live with Bettina."

Bettina's closing plea were words addressed to all of us: "What did they give me to go out and survive with? Nothing but emptiness and anger.

"There's a lot of young kids out there that we can still save, for the ones I couldn't, the ones that are dead now. Society, hang your head in shame, because you people are the ones contributing to this – you are accepting it. 'Let's let the professionals handle it.' No one is speaking up.

"A main reason a lot of women don't make it is because it is very lonely out here. There aren't a lot of people ready to help. Right now people can get away with saying, 'Well, we didn't know.' My main reason for telling people about my life is so they will know. Once you know, and don't do anything, then you are responsible.

"I write to 22 women in jail and share with them my struggle. I am trying to show them all it can be done. But we need outside help too."

CRUMBLING WALLS: WHY PRISONS FAIL

*   *   *   *   *

Although the subject of minority groups and prisons could fill volumes, we will include just one other topic here: Capital Punishment. It may seem strange to include this issue in a section on minorities, but we do it with the positive intent to underline the fact that Capital Punishment is even more reserved for minorities than are prisons. As the article below shows, it is no coincidence that the very moderate National Association for the Advancement of Colored People (NAACP) has put up a heroic struggle against Capital Punishment for decades: they know exactly whose necks are on the line.

THE NOOSE, THE CHAIR, AND THE NEEDLE[3]

"Capital Punishment means them without
the capital gets the punishment

This witty button might be funny if if weren't for the fact that polls show that 68% of Canadians favour a return to hanging, and soundings indicate about 2/3 of our present Parliament, given a free vote, would endorse a return to Capital Punishment. Gloomy figures for those of us who don't want to see Canada join the U.S. and Turkey as the only western nations carrying out the death penalty.

The good news is that the same polls show these beliefs are based largely on an absence of accurate information:

–80% of Canadians have not read anything on the issue:
–University of Toronto Criminologists Doob and Roberts found Canadians believe the violent crime rate 7 times what it actually is, and that the murder rate has been increasing since 1976 (it has not).

The answer then appears to be in education and lobbying, by those of us who know and care about the issue.

Arguments Against The Death Penalty:

There are six major reasons for opposing the death penalty:

1) DISCRIMINATION:
Everywhere, racial minorities and the poor are far more likely than others to get executed.

2) MISTAKES:
Beyond a shadow of a doubt, many innocent people have been executed.

3) LOTTERY:
Any way you look at the figures, the tiny proportion of those executed compared to the numbers of victims of all kinds of social ills, including victims of murder, makes Capital Punishment the most barbaric lottery of them all.

4) MORAL-RELIGIOUS:
Regardless of anything else, we cannot practice Capital Punishment because of what it does to us when we engage in willful, premeditated social murder.

5) DETERRENCE:
There is no evidence that deterrence works.

6) POLITICAL OPPRESSION:
Amnesty International and others oppose Capital Punishment because around the world more people are executed for their political or religious beliefs or behaviour than for any other reason.

Discrimination

Supreme Court Justice Douglas in the U.S.A. put it this way: "One searches in vain for the execution of any member of the affluent strata of our society." Rep. Conyers points out that in the U.S., the chances are 3-10 times greater of being executed for killing a white person than for killing a black person. More than 90% of those on death rows could not afford to hire their own lawyers at the trial. Lest anyone imagine that discrimination is foreign to Canadian courts, my own 1982 study of the bail courts in Toronto showed substantial racial discrimination making it harder for blacks than for whites to be released on bail; and a number of studies cited in the recent Canadian Dimension article on Natives and prisons show rank discrimination by Canadian courts against Native people.

There is no question that if we reinstitute Capital Punishment, we will not be selecting the nastiest and most dangerous Canadians to execute: we will be executing almost exclusively: POOR people, BLACK people, NATIVE people, and OTHER MINORITIES. It is no coincidence that the otherwise very moderate National Association for the Advancement of Colored People (NAACP) in the U.S.A. has pioneered in the fight against Capital Punishment for decades: they know perfectly well whose necks are on the line. For myself, even if all other arguments were nonexistent, I could not condone Capital Punishment, knowing it has operated everywhere and at all times as the ultimate expression of racial hatred and economic oppression.

Mistakes

A recent American Civil Liberties Union study cites 343 cases in the U.S. history where people were clearly wrongful convicted of offences punishable by death. Twenty-five of these people were actually executed. University of Florida Criminologist Radelet identified over 100 innocent individuals who were at one time condemned to die. In Canada, in the past two years, both John Wildman and Donald Marshall have been released from prison after serving years for murders they did not commit: had we had Capital Punishment, they too might have been dead.

To all of this, Ernest Van den Haag, a Fordham Professor of Jurisprudence, says the "Infrequency of improper executions...buttresses the case for Capital Punishment...25 wrongful executions, if true, is a very acceptable number." He adds that playing golf or football causes accidental death, and concludes triumphantly that we have in these few errors of Capital Punishment, "A net gain in justice." I suppose we are all entitled to our own ideas of justice, and Hitler's eugenics were based on a kindred theory that a few innocent lives and a few civil liberties were well worth sacrificing for the greater good of society. But I don't seriously think many Dimension readers are willing to pay the price Professor Van den Haag thinks so acceptable for the dubious benefits Capital Punishments offers.

Lottery

The best way to explain this argument is to look at some figures:

Of 20,000 U.S. homicides a year, fewer than 150 people will be given a death sentence.

The chances of receiving the death penalty are many times greater in certain states, under certain Judges, than others.

Far from being any systematic form of justice, the death penalty is a lottery, and one of the few in which the underprivileged are favoured to win–but what they win is a ticket to state supplied death.

Another really significant way of looking at the situation is this: if it is violent and unnatural death we fear, our chances of losing a loved one to drunk driving are 2 1/2 times as great as to murder; and we are 6 times as likely to lose someone to an industrial accident as to murder. If we seriously believe Capital Punishment for murder is the best mode of prevention, who's for Capital Punishment for drunk drivers?...or for industrial tycoons with lax safety codes? Either one would make more sense as a social protection, if you're looking for safety against the odds, and you believe punishment deters.

Deterrence

Since the abolition of Capital Punishment in Canada, the homicide rate has decreased from 3.09 per 100,000 to 2.74. Comparisons of neighboring states in the U.S. with and without Capital Punishment show no consistent differences. My own favourite story on deterrence is that the reason they had to discontinue the public hangings of pickpockets in 17th century England was not humanity: there were too many pickpockets operating in the crowds watching the public hangings. In short, there just is no clear evidence to support the belief that Capital Punishment deters others from murder. And this is more logical when one considers that contrary to popular belief, the average murderer is not a fiend lurking in a dark alley premeditating brutal murder, but a member of one's own household or close friend, who acts out of spontaneous passion. Murderers don't add up the odds and play their cards rationally: they act out of spontaneous emotions in situations of high pressure. Calculating the temper of the local judiciary, the current legislation, and the odds of apprehension are just not part of the thinking of very many of them.

Political Oppression

As I write this, countless people around the world are being imprisoned, tortured, and otherwise oppressed for their political beliefs. Many will come out and do great things for their countries and for humanity. Some will not come out, for they will have been executed. As long as Capital Punishment exists, it will be used as an instrument of political oppression and as a means of exterminating one's opposition. Funny how we always think we are immune from this at home, but the use of the state as a weapon of oppression is inherent in our inability to know objectively when we are doing it. I remember one prisoner in Ontario who was transferred to maximum security because a poem which he wrote was read at an Easter service, and it was critical of the prison.

Among the people who would have been spared had the state not thought it had the right to take life officially are: Socrates, Jesus Christ, Joan of Arc, Martin Niemoller, and Thomas A Becket. Pretty good company.

The Other Side Of The Coin: Fear and Revenge

Ranged against all these arguments are the powerful forces of our fear of violence in ourselves, in others, in the world around us, and our desire for revenge against all the ills that beset us in life. Capital Punishment is one of the few socially acceptable outlets for these emotions. It is all right to project our fear and our anger on these few socially selected scapegoats and pray God and country to blast them to Hell. But if we are truly concerned about violence there are some much more obvious and effective remedies than Capital Punishment:

1) GUN CONTROL:
Professor Waller estimates even the weak gun control laws of 1976 in the U.S.A. have saved over 500 lives.

2) FAMILY CRISIS INTERVENTION:

Which could intervene in potentially violent situations, and could also identify and help children on their way toward being future helpless purveyors of violence.

3) REDUCTION OF OVERT TV VIOLENCE:

The National Coalition on Violent Entertainment estimates this generation of TV viewers will see 600 times more assaults, 500 times more rapes, and 300 times more murders than their predecessors. This increases perception of our society as violent, and fear and anger about violence. A study by Dr. Gerbner of Annenberg School of Communications has shown that heavy TV viewers are more right-wing than light viewers because of this distorted view of reality. Moreover, over 2000 separate studies link media violence to negative effects on children.

4) MEANINGFUL VICTIM SERVICES:

Victims do need help, as Howard Zehr has said:
- Recognition that what has happened to them is tragic and wrong;
- Release from blame;
- People who will listen patiently;
- Opportunities to grieve;
- Compensation for damages and burdens;
- Right to information about the facts.

With these supports, victims need not turn to blind vengeance, and more can take the kind of path of the amazing Marie Deans, who has sublimated her grief over a family murder by visiting and ministering to over 200 men and women on death row.

What We Can Do

Despite the odds quoted at the beginning of this article, we can remain an abolitionist state in Canada. Above all, we need to let our MPs, newspapers, and the public know there are those of us who don't want to step back toward blind vengeance. Unless you're poor, black, and unlucky, the life you save probably will not be your own. Why not save somebody else's?

This short tour of the subject of prisons and minority groups illustrates the same point over and over again: prisons ARE racism, they ARE the oppression of the poor by the rich. One of the most powerful reasons why prisons have got to go is that they are an extreme manifestation of the corruption of power. We human beings have two opposing forces in us at all times: the power of transcending selfishness through growth in caring for one another; and the power of selfish goals and abuse of power to take over our lives, and blot out the perception of others as part of us. Prisons have to go because they make all of us less human, they blunt our ability to see one another as all part of the human race, and they destroy what is best in those outside the prisons subtly but just as effectively as they destroy those within.

NOTES

1.   *Canadian Dimension*, Vol. 19, No. 5, December 1985, pp7–8.

2.   Reprinted from *Canadian Dimensions*, Vol. 20, No. 8, February 1987, pp 10–12.

3.   First printed in slightly altered form in *Canadian Dimension*, Vol. 20, No.3, May 1986, pp 6–8.

PART III

THE VISION BEYOND
THE WALLS:

TRUE ALTERNATIVES

Writing in 1980 on behalf of our Quaker Committee on Jails and Justice, I said: "Just as pacifism goes far beyond passivism, and the true pacifist must work toward 'taking away the occasion of all wars,' so must the prison abolitionists go as beyond calling for abolition of the prison system... We recognize that the call for abolition of prisons is meaningless rhetoric unless we are willing to take the responsibility for demonstrating living alternatives for every   prisoner group."

This burning conviction led me to devote a decade of my life to the founding and start-up of four different alternatives to prison:

1) Toronto Bail Program

2) Toronto Bail Residence (Halfway House)

3) My Brother's Place (Halfway House)

4) St. Stephen's Conflict Resolution Service

This section includes six short presentations about alternatives to prisons. First is a general paper on "Creative Alternatives To Prisons." I wrote this years old as part of the educational effort which led to the adoption of a prison abolition stance, with total consensus, by Canadian Quakers. Since then it has been widely circulated and reprinted. Although a few parts of it are a little dated, it still presents the clearest short summary of existing alternatives that I know of, and as such, is a logical opening for this section on alternatives.

The next three sections discuss in more depth the three kinds of alternatives I have been most involved in creating: pretrial release through the Bail Program; transitional housing through group homes; and the role of community mediation services in dealing with problems before they ever reach courts.

After these, a short section follows on the inevitable question: What would you do with the few violent/sexual offenders? Finally, a summary section on alternatives discusses the vital issue of what makes an alternative a true alternative, instead of merely a prison in the community with less visible chains.

1.
CREATIVE ALTERNATIVES TO PRISONS: WHAT WORKS BETTER?

"OK, you've convinced me," people sometimes say pretty quickly. "Prisons are not the greatest. They breed crime and bitterness, destroy people who work and live in them, and it's not nice to cage your fellow humans. They cost more than the best university education, while giving appalling results.

"But in the face of rising crime, are there any alternatives that make any more sense?"

This little pamphlet is a very short answer to that question. The bibliography at the end points out some of the fuller answers available.

Alternatives To Prisons

Alternatives to prisons are not just a visionary future ideal being talked about by a few imaginative dreamers. All the following alternatives listed are now in practice – most of them in Ontario, and their use only needs to be expanded and refined. Some, like probation and parole, date back to the 19th century, but most are relatively recent, and represent a growing recognition by the community that WE deserve something better than prisons.

Creative alternatives now being used include:

1) Supervision in the community, including probation, parole, and bail supervision.

2) Diversion.

3) Community service work orders.

4) Fine option programs.

5) Restitution.

6) Victim-offender reconciliation programs and community dispute mediation centres.

7) Community Resource Centres; Halfway Homes; Therapeutic Communities.

8) Immediate TAP (temporary absence pass).

1) COMMUNITY SUPERVISION PROGRAMS

Probation goes back to the remarkable efforts of a Boston cobbler, John Augustus, who spent much time in the courts and became so involved in the plight of the drunks and poor he found there that he personally paid many fines. By 1858 he had bailed out 1152 men and 794 women and girls! He had also befriended over 3000 other friendless women. For all of which service he was subjected to a great deal of caustic criticism.

The greatest difference among *probation, parole, and bail supervision* is in when they occur in the legal process:

BAIL SUPERVISION is to keep people out of jail with responsible supervision while they are awaiting trial, before guilt or innocence has been decided. Without bail supervision, the poor go to jail while those with resources get out on money bails. Without it also, punishment in the form of weeks or months of incarceration occurs even before trial.

PROBATION is an order of the Judge after conviction. It is a decision that this person, now found guilty, should be placed in the community with supervision and guidance to avoid any future trouble.

PAROLE, last in order, comes when someone has served part of a prison sentence and is a way of releasing him gradually toward independence to the community, before all the maximum prison time has passed. It provides the community a measure of protection, and for the parolee, helps in making a difficult transition to a hostile community.

Community supervision programs have their weaknesses: such powers of supervision can be abused, or more often, with too large caseloads, neglected. But they are over the decades the best established alternative to prisons, and have proved themselves in thousands of lives, which have been helped toward a better future, instead of being started down the destructive slide of imprisonment. Supervision programs relate people to other community services, including: welfare, drug and alcohol counselling, rehab, emergency and longterm housing assistance, personal counselling, and education and job upgrading.

2) DIVERSION

Diversion refers to programs which divert the whole problem before it ever reaches the courts. Most diversion programs deal with first offenders, many with minor offenders, and referrals often come largely from the police themselves. The idea of diversion is to spare the person the whole criminal process – which is in many cases the process of making a person feel and become a criminal. Instead, he is told about diversion, and given the choice of working with the diversion centre or of choosing the court route.

In diversion, the accused person and the diversion worker begin by his accepting responsibility for the alleged action, and go on to plan together what should be done in response. A number of appropriate choices are discussed whether educational, work, or compensatory, and the client is then encouraged to go out into the community, explore these options, and come back to the worker with his own plan which they can discuss. Court processes stigmatize, stereotype, inspire guilt, and deprive the accused of creative initiative. Diversion has opposite effects when well applied: it encourages initiative and response by the accused, and helps him work through guilt feelings constructively.

Unfortunately, as long as punishment is a primary motive, diversion will continue to be little used because it is not perceived as sufficiently punishing.

3) COMMUNITY SERVICE WORK ORDERS

Like several other kinds of alternatives, CSOs are usually given along with probation, as one condition of a probation order.

Instead of incarcerating an offender, he is given probation along with an order to put in so many hours without pay doing some community service: delivering meals on wheels for the elderly, shovelling snow, cleaning parks, working in children's centres...Good work habits, constructive use of leisure time, new relationships are only some of the byproducts all contributing to a more positive self-image. Whereas prisons cost at least $50 per day, administration of CSOs costs about $3 a day.

4) FINE OPTION PROGRAMS

These programs in Manitoba and Saskatchewan were started mainly for Native people because so many of them given a "$50 or 5 days" choice end up having to serve the 5 days. The programs are not limited to Native people, however.

Fine option programs offer people ways to earn the money to pay their fine, thus gaining work experience and contributing to the community and their own future, instead of costing the community $250 while destroying their own initiative still more in jail.

5) RESTITUTION

In restitution programs, the offender repays the victim through the court, as part of a probation order. Restitution "gives the victim back his crime." Many legal processes remove the victim from the action, leave him entangled in legalities with no compensation, little help or interpretation, so that what follows his original victimization is sometimes worse than the crime itself was. Restitution turns attention back to the victim, restores to him some compensation, usually monetary, for loss. It also gives the offender a chance to earn and repay honestly what he stole or destroyed, and a sense of proportion related to his action. The lack of a connection between a small theft and months in prison deprives most offenders of an understanding of justice, and leaves them feeling a sense of having been wronged. Restitution relates what they did to what they must do.

6) VICTIM - OFFENDER RECONCILIATION AND COMMUNITY DISPUTE MEDIATION CENTRES

Victim-offender reconciliation programs bring victim and offender together in an effort to heal wounds, and bring something constructive for both out of a mutually negative start. A homeowner whose door was vandalized may after discussion agree to have the offender work on repairing it. The victim of course must agree to participate in such a program, but as in restitution and other alternatives, the victim's suffering is dealt with far more positively than by the usual legal process. Meeting with the victim cuts away for the offender the impersonality of urban life, and he perceives that there are real people hurt by this kind of behaviour. Victims in turn have their fear and anxiety diminished and their compassion aroused by meeting with and seeing how down and out most offenders are.

Community dispute mediation centres take the matter one step further back, and can deal with disputes between parties without saying "you are the offender, you are the victim." Many matters that end up in court with one person charging another are really matters of mutual dispute, which such a centre can try to resolve by discussion between the parties with a mediator.

7) CRCS, HALFWAY HOMES

Community Resource Centres are used in Ontario for prisoners serving the last part of their sentences who can get jobs in the community. Though still serving sentence and subject to control in every way, they go out into the community to work, and are allowed a good deal of freedom on weekends and evenings, once they show their reliability. Run by social agencies on behalf of the Ministry of Corrections, CRCs are a very constructive step toward de-institutionalizing people gradually.

Halfway homes are in some ways similar in the provision of sympathetic counsellors along with some fairly firm house rules. But in a halfway house, a person usually stays voluntarily, and can leave when he wishes, unless it is a term of his parole or other court order.

Therapeutic communities include drug and alcoholic facilities, mental hospitals, and psychiatric institutions. Few of the public realize how thin is the border between mental illness and legal guilt, and that much the same population goes back and forth between the jails (with minor offences) and the mental hospitals.

8) IMMEDIATE TAPs

Temporary absence passes may be used to enable a prisoner to go to a funeral, have a family visit after months of incarceration, or try out a parole arrangement proposed. The immediate TAP enables people to keep their jobs, serving their sentence on weekends, or weekends and nights.

What About The Dangerous Ones?

If all these good things exist, and are in practice, then what are we worried about? And anyhow, are any of them relevant for the really serious offender?

Although all exist, none are as extensively used as they might be, and one reason is that courts respond in sentencing to the wishes, fears, and desires for vengeance that they hear coming from you and me.

Opinions on who IS a serious offender, and what proportion of the prison population are "dangerous" will vary, of course. But very few people who have met the prison population believe that a majority of them are violent. Most volunteers, after their first time inside come away exclaiming, "But where are the real CRIMINALS!?" – so little do the longhaired, loudmouthed, irritating but innocuous youth they met fit the public stereotype of a vicious criminal.

Nonetheless, there are a few, call it 10% as most social agencies do, or 20 or 30 as some of the more conservative groups do – who are truly dangerous. Don't we need prisons for them?

Opinions vary on what to do with the few, but no one believes that mixing them with the young, inexperienced offender does anyone any good. It is this mixing in the whole prison setting that makes many of the 10% hardcore. But even without prisons to do it, a few people become so damaged by life that they are dangerous. Public protection is needed, certainly, but is public revenge? Surely a very different kind of custodial facility could meet this need for the few.

Future Alternatives

If these alternatives are so good, why do we still have prisons – and crime? What other alternatives could we have that aren't here yet?

Of course, many of the alternatives are not so well developed or so fully used as they could be. Fines, for instance, if used, should be more closely related to income. A $50 fine for one person may be a joke; for another, a tragedy. Sentencing in general should be much more closely related to the actual offence. Better civil settlements for financial disputes would be more satisfactory to the people involved, and result in fewer financial issues being dealt with – often inappropriately – in the Criminal courts.

Some newer and more progressive alternatives need a wider chance: victim-offender reconciliation, diversion, and community resource centres. An important future step would be community intervention courts similar to community mediation dispute centres, refocussing conflict so that all share responsibility, and trying to identify and resolve conflicts rather than labelling people "criminals" and "victims."

The consistently high correlation between incarceration rates and unemployment points out the value of alternatives focussing on job skills and employment – such as the New Careers scheme. Creative experiments in Great Britain and elsewhere have virtually closed down institutions for youth by integrating these youth into the community.

A television show some years ago portrayed a community which had a lottery every year. In the lottery one of its finest youth was chosen for death. A stranger who entered the community and questioned the necessity for the lottery was condemned and driven out. Our lotteries are not quite so random – but they do select from our youth those to be isolated and further destroyed. Have we the vision and daring to try more creative alternatives?

2.
TORONTO BAIL PROGRAM

One of the special opportunites of my life, thanks to Art Daniels, Ruth Pitman, and Connie Mahaffy, then of the Ontario Ministry of Corrections was that of founding and directing for nearly four years the large and exciting Toronto Bail Program. Helping keep hundreds of people from pretrial detention, the program was pioneering work. The process and some of the results are described below.

TORONTO BAIL PROGRAM[1]

In 1979 the Ontario Ministry of Corrections was faced with some hard choices. Studies indicated that over half the admittances to jails were remand prisoners, persons waiting for trial. The number of remands was rising rapidly, and four institutions were operating at over 100% of their daily population capacity.

Faced with a choice between building more jails and launching new community alternatives, Ontario Ministry of Corrections chose to follow its basic goal of promoting community alternatives wherever possible. A number of private agencies were interested in the development of pretrial alternatives in Ontario. An agency in Kitchener-Waterloo called "Youth in Conflict With the Law" had already been experimenting with Bail Supervision as an alternative in some cases. The John Howard Societies of St. Catherines and Hamilton were already asking the Ministry of Corrections to fund Bail Programs, and the Salvation Army and the Elizabeth Fry Societies were also interested in the idea.

Two Remedies: Verification and Supervision

The problem of people detained in custody unnecessarily fell into two categories:

1) Those temporarily detained who could be released on their own recognizance or to sureties more quickly if fuller and more accurate information were available to bail courts earlier.

2) Those with bails set but who were detained in custody because of the absence of a surety with means to satisfy the bail. That is, those detained basically by poverty of resources supporting them.

Verification was designed to deal with the first problem, and *Supervision* with the second.

Verification

The Ministry of Correctional Services statistic indicated that slightly more than half of remand prisoners admitted to the jails would stay 7 days or less. The logical question this suggested was: if these people were suitable for release within 7 days, why couldn't they be released immediately, if adequate information were available to the court at the very first bail hearing? To meet this problem, the same solution was proposed which had been pioneered in VERA in New York City, and in other bail programs in England and the United States: Verification.

In verification, trained interviewers interview accused persons as soon as possible after the police have finished their interrogation. However, the bail verification interviewer avoids any questions pertaining to the alleged offence, and concentrates instead entirely on information regarding the accused person's bail status:

1)   What are his community ties, length of time in the community, family supports, other potential sureties, general stability in the area.

2)   Does he/she have a suitable place to come out to; if so, how appropriate, stable, and supportive is it? (A known center of drug trade at one extreme, vs. a well-established stable family home at the other). If there is no current stable address, can the interviewer and client agree on a suitable alternative?

3)   Does the accused have a job or is he/she involved in schooling currently? Can appropriate plans or referrals be made in either of these areas?

4)   How does the record of the accused relate to bail status, including especially the history of Fails to Appear and Fails to Comply, and the reason for these and attitude toward them by the accused?

5)   Are there identifiable problems of alcohol or drug abuse or mental illness for which the court will want some suitable recommendations if the accused is to be released?

6)   Is the accused already on some form of bail release, or on probation or parole?

Obviously, the verification interview could in theory be a one to two hour depth interview, if it were to cover all this well. In reality, without verifiers, all of the above is covered as far as it is covered at all by duty counsel,[1] as a 3-5 minute interview which must also include a lot of questions about the alleged offence and whether the person wishes to plead guilty at this point.

It is easy to see from this that a verifier who can spend a little more time on this area and do some phoning afterward to confirm information given can serve a vital function for the court. Even the verifier, owing to pressures of time and space in the few hours between arrest and the first hearing, is usually restricted to interviews of 10-15 minutes, and often to 5 minutes. But with training and experience, a surprising amount can be elicited in the verification interview, and checked out in the short time before court.

Supervision

In Canada, bail bondsmen are illegal, and although a few operate sub rosa, they are not a widespread phenomenon. While this is on the whole an improvement over all the potential abuses of the bail bondsmen system in many American jurisdictions, it leaves the accused person who lacks much financial resource in the community with no alternative. Either he can come up with a surety worth the whole amount of the bail, or he stays in jail.

Yet the purpose of the surety system is not to raise money, but to insure suitable community supervision of the accused, and to give him an incentive to appear in the court at the proper times. Two precedents[2] in Canadian law indicate it is a violation of the intent of the court for a bail set to operate as a detention order. Yet despite that, the jails are full of people to whom that happens. Even with our program operating, there are currently about 90 people in Toronto jails with bails set, for whom our staff are phoning sureties. For some of those 90, an appropriate surety will not come forward. What then?

Without a suitable alternative, the pre-trial system becomes just one more place where the law for the poor is much heavier than the law for the rich. To take a strong illustration: two young men in the past three years spent 3 weeks each in our Toronto Jail while waiting for trial. Each of them had a $10 bail set, but no one to come forward for that petty amount. The injustice and inefficiency of this is so obvious it is appalling. And incidentally, the community footed the bill of over $1000 each for keeping them in jail that long in this absurd situation.

The Judges in setting those bails didn't want the $10. They wanted someone to supervise the young men in question, to give the court a reasonable probability these accused would appear in court without major further trouble. If this is the basic function of the surety, why can't professional staff do it for the poor as part of their official function? This is the idea behind bail supervision.

If an accused person appears suitable for release on surety bail, but verification indicates a suitable surety does not exist, then bail supervision is the logical alternative. The Bail Program would recommend to the Court that the accused be released on his own recognizance, but with the provision that he report to and be subject to the supervision of the Bail Program. Some have argued that this too discrimates against the poor: if the accused had had friends to bail him out, he would have been spared this reporting. But in fact, legal traditions indicate that a surety is historically "a jailer in the community" and has the responsibility for community supervision of the accused. So long as the Bail Program supervision unit also takes the role of a positive friendly supervision, it is the nearest equivalent we can create.

Target Groups

Accused persons arrested by the Police may initially be divided into two groups: those who are released on their own undertaking without the necessity for a bail hearing, and those who are held for a show-cause bail hearing. This latter group are the target group for bail verification, but the target group for supervision is very much narrower. In essence, a number of possible disposals are considered by the Court at bail hearings, and these fall into four categories:

1)   Those released by the Court on their own undertaking or recognizance.

2)   Those released by the Court on condition that they report to the Police.

3)   Those who receive a Detention Order.

4)   Those who are appropriate for surety bail.

Those who can provide the appropriate surety are not the concern of Bail Program workers - it is those who cannot who are the target group for supervision.

Challenge of Metro Toronto

For awhile the Ministry of Corrections (Community Branch) was uncertain what to do about a program in Metropolitan Toronto. Since Toronto was the largest urban area in Ontario, it represented the largest challenge. One of the biggest questions people planning the new venture asked themselves was: how can we be sure of focussing on the TARGET GROUP and only on the target group? So many efforts at alternatives had, it seemed, been used by the courts as an add-on to prison instead of an alternative, as was intended. In offering bail supervision for those who qualified for release on bail terms, but could not raise surety bail, Ministry of Correctional Services did not wish to find itself funding a vast program of supervision, including all kinds of people formerly released on their own recognizance, or simply reporting weekly to the Police Bail and Parole Unit for a sign-in.

At first the Ministry of Correctional Services hesitated to launch a program in Metro Toronto. The largest single group of those arrested were now being released by the police without even a bail hearing. Those released on their own undertaking at court included many thousands more, and about 1800 were reproting to the Police Bail and Parole Unit. None of these people were the responsibility of the Ministry of Correctional Services, and the last thing they wanted was to fund a program which added surveillance and supervision to a large number of accused persons already on the street without any special program. If a program could be directed solely at the target group for supervision, those appropriate for surety bail but who lacked an appropriate surety, it would be worth it. But could they take the chance?

A reported 20% rise in the remand statistics in Toronto made them decide it was worth it. But because of the size of this program and the challenges it faced, the Ministry of Correctional Services decided to be personally involved in starting it out. Other Bail Programs in Ontario were funded by the Ministry of Correctional Services but run entirely by private agencies. In Toronto, MCS asked their Provincial Coordinator for Pretrial Services, Connie

Mahaffy, to design a model program with Verification and Supervision. They also invited proposals from the three most interested private agencies: John Howard, E. Fry and the Salvation Army. The agencies and the MCS then sat down together to work out a stategy.

New Experiment

What emerged was a new experiment in cooperation. The Ministry of Correctional Services would plan the basic design through Ms. Mahaffy, and it would also hire a project manager and secretary for the program. The three private agencies would receive funding for seconding one worker each to the program. MCS also applied to our Federal Government, Ministry of the Solicitor General, to hire young people under a Job Corps program at minimum wage to help with verification.

A pilot program was run on this basis for 7 months, at which point MCS was committed to its policy of "privatization." The project was working well, and the three private agencies combined to become a Board of Management for the new agency, with one representative from the community at large. In itself, this was a unique develoopment, as these three agencies had never before collaborated so closely on a program. But our Board continues to function effectively and cooperatively.

Challenges in Program Development

Our own experience and my visits to other programs suggest that there are a number of common problems to be solved in beginning a Bail Program. These include:

1) *Access* to newly arrested persons.

2) *Space* needs for the program.

3) *Public Relations.* Arranging for the program to be known by all parts of the justice system, and to achieve the necessary balance and fairness for acceptance by all.

4) *Civil Liberties* issues surrounding verification.

5) *Standard Agency Problems:* hiring, training of personnel, information flow, design of standard forms, budget and salary arrangements, etc.

6) *Enforcement* issues and procedures on supervision.

7) *Community Resources:* liaison and development.

We will discuss each of these areas briefly, and how we worked with them.

Access to Newly Arrested Persons

This is a problem to most but not all Bail Programs initially. A great deal depends on who is starting the program, and what their relationship is to those responsible for holding in custody newly arrested person. In our case, the program was being sponsored by private agencies and the Ministry of Corrections, while the Police hold in their direct custody most persons waiting for their first bail hearing. Therefore, we had to gain police cooperation for access to these persons.

Police in charge of court cells were reluctant for two reasons to give us access. First of all, there was a natural tendency for Police to view the program at first as one more scheme for putting directly out on the street all the offenders they had just gone to a great deal of trouble to arrest and hold. Secondly, security concerns about the court cells led the Police to consider that the less traffic in and out the better, and their desire was to cut down the number of persons with access, not add a large new agency to the traffic pattern.

Changing these problems has been a gradual process, with much credit due to those Police who have labored patiently with us in our growing pains, and have learned to understand the program as it has unfolded. At present we have reasonably satisfactory access arrangements as follows:

(a) In all suburban courts and one downtown court, where facilities are modern and through a glass, our verifiers go into court cells along with the duty counsels, and do the verification interviewing.

(b)   Because of the very bad security setup in the largest downtown court, the prisoners held here are interviewed by us in the stations where they are arrested, between 3 and 6 a.m. each morning.

(c)   When a candidate for supervision has been missed in this process for whatever reason, the bail court judge can order our worker to interview the potential client, and access is given accordingly.

Space Needs for the Program

Our operation is housed entirely in courthouses, with all the pros and cons implied in that. We enjoy rent-free facilities so convenient to the court that the job of getting clients to court for appearances is much easier than if we were located elsewhere. On the other hand, we have to struggle for space along with other competing agencies and court personnel, and sometimes a lot of our administrative energies are spent on this rather unsatisfying task.

This area does point out one interest facet of the program. Although we are a service to the courts (Attorney General's responsibility) we are funded and sponsored by the Ministry of Correctional Services. As the Attorney General controls court space assignments, we are delicately balanced between the two ministries at times.

Public Relations

This is one of the more challenging and interesting problems. In our very adversarial system, a new agency walks a tightrope amongst all the conflicting demands and suspicions of the rival groups. To meet this problem, we established early a "Liaison Committee" since renamed an "Advisory Committee." It includes two jail superintendents, representatives of the defence bar, the Crown, duty counsel, our own Board, probation, police, and our central Ministry of Corrections. We would have included a representative of the bench, but the Chief Judge felt this inappropriate. However, even without a judge, the Committee provided a powerful two-way link to nearly all elements in the justice system.

Problems and misunderstandings were fed back to us before they became acute. Our own problems were relayed to other groups as needed. Best of all, solutions to issues such as the wording of delicate questions on the verification interview were hammered out in a group with all parties represented.

Even as I wrote this, a major issue is being dealt with by representatives of Defence and Crown on our Advisory Committee, who are working on an undertaking by the Crown not to use information from verification in prosecution for guilt at the trial stage.

These high-powered meetings are not only a highlight for the program, but other points of mutual interest have been worked out by the members because this is one of the few settings where all these parties come together.

We have also done a lot of public speaking, writing of articles for related newsletters, held one dramatic large open-house, entertained numerous visitors to the program, and had several press articles done on the program. But mostly, public relations is day to day plugging, stopping a crown in the hall and explaining the program to him, or making an appointment with a judge whose responses indicate he doesn't fully understand the target group we are seeking. One of our most enjoyable evenings was an invitation to speak with the Supreme Court Justices of Ontario, who were very warm and receptive to the program. Following this, they invited us to cover all Supreme Court Bail reviews for the program.

Civil Liberties Issues

Last year I visited the Pretrial Information Center in Washington, D.C., and confirmed the suspicion I had by then that any Bail Program worth its salt will sooner or later encounter this problem. Verification by non-legal personnel who are not privileged (can be subpoenaed) raises some serious questions about the civil liberties of the accused. He/she is peculiarly vulnerable, and even with warnings may divulge all kinds of damaging information to the first sympathetic person encountered since arrest.

But if the service is for the whole court, and if it is to have credibility for the whole court, the information, most of which is potentially damaging to the accused, must be shared with the whole court. It is a basic dilemma of verification. After a few false starts we came to the following terms, and all parties seemed reasonably happy for the time being with them:

1) Obviously, the verifier does not in any way or at any time ask or listen to any information on the current charge. The court docket lists the charge; beyond that, the verifier stays totally out of that area.

2) A carefully worded warning is given the client at the beginning, and a consent to be interviewed obtained, which informs him/her that they don't have to be interviewed and that information about the charge itself can be used against them, and that the information they give will be shared with the Crown.

3) A large section of verification information which is valuable but delicate was moved from the main part of the interview to a confidential section solely for use of the Bail Program. This includes information on previous record, health conditions and aliases.

4) It was agreed by all parties including the police that no verification information would be shared directly with the police, but only with the Crown and defence.

5) The written material to be shared with the court is distilled in a short, carefully-worded, one-page summary sheet after verification calls have been made.

Standard Agency Problems

Since problems of staff selection, hiring, training, information flow, and so on are standard items, I will not go into these except to say that obviously they take up a great deal of the administrative energy of any program. One highlight of our efforts has been a very active volunteer component and a very open, exciting office where clients, volunteers, visitors and staff mingle in an atmosphere full of surprises.

RUTH MORRIS

Enforcement Issues and Procedures on Supervision

A surety makes a commitment to the court to notify authorities if he/she has reason to believe the accused is fleeing. A Bail Supervision Program has similar obligations. We have to make it clear to our clients that it is a condition of their release that they report to us, keep in touch, and obey all conditions of bail. In addition to discussing this as part of selection, we sign a contract on it during the initial intake interview when they are first released.

Obviously our staff, who are in this work because they believe completely in trying to help our clients, find this the least happy part of their work. Personally, as a prison abolitionist I am certainly not delighted at being responsible for putting some people back into custody, and/or laying charges on people. But as a Quaker who believes in absolute truthfulness with all parties, I know that I have agreed with the Court in each case to practice enforcement as the price of the individual's release to our care and so in all truth we have to practice it. That is why it is essential to convey this to the client.

There are other problems with enforcement though. There are two provisions of the law under which we can lay Fail to Comply Charges. The more usual one, 127CCC, actually involves a charge laid by us. But the one the police and we have agreed on, 457CCC, simply involves taking the individual back to court to say "This hasn't worked, let's re-evaluate," and a charge is not automatic. It is more like a surety withdrawing his bail, which may occur for a variety of reasons. However, the Justices of the Peace are less aware of this provision, and have been reluctant to allow us to use it, so we are still working on negotiations on this one, after 1 1/2 years of supervision.

In short, enforcement involves the cooperation and various reactions of the clients, supervisors, police, and Justices of the Peace. The standards have to keep the Crown, police, and Defence bar content, not to mention our Board, staff and clients. In general, we make every effort to notify and locate absent clients ourselves, and even have some volunteers who go to addresses and chase them down for us. Our clients come from backgrounds where times, dates and locations are blurred in contrast to the rigid standards of our courts, and we try to bridge the gaps and bring them closer in every way.

132

Community Resources: Liaison and Development

In order to do an adequate job of both verification and supervision, it is essential for our staff to have at their fingertips a knowledge of a wide variety of community resources. In verification, often our ability to provide a suitable address for a person to come out to, or some other community agency which will give the person some guidance or support, may permit a release on his own recognizance or to a surety. And in supervision, appropriate use of all community resources is an absolute key to success.

In the downtown courts, roughly 50% of our clients have no fixed address when we get them. Good relations and communication with all the free and cheap hostels is essential for dealing with this problem alone. In addition, since most hostels have a 7 or 14 day limit, we have to keep moving the individual unless he is able to enter employment, a state which many of them are not ready for. The hostels also have no day program and the client (mostly rootless youth lacking in lifeskills) is left on the downtown streets all day to get in trouble, if other appropriate referrals are not made and followed. Moreover, our clients have, of course, a certain degree of facility for violating rules and getting thrown out of residences.

The lack of appropriate housing is therefore one acute problem. I have been very involved in working on this one, and we have just received a letter of intent from the Ontario Ministry of Corrections for the opening of a 14-bed bail residence next month, with a day program to include lifeskills, leisure time facilities, and a job referral program. We have also been involved with the court chaplains and other related groups in starting an umbrella organization called Shelter Now Network. SNN has a committee working on a clearinghouse for all persons involved with the correctional system with housing needs; the bail residence came out of one of its committees, and another committee is working on establishing another much needed Halfway House. Another staff member, Bill O'Neill, is exploring possibilities for a residence for those with drug addiction problems; and our Newmarket staff person, Olivia Wilson, has been instrumental in getting an active committee going there to establish a residence for people on bail, probation, parole, or in similar need.

Another major problem of course is jobs. But many of our clients lack the basic lifeskills needed even to apply, let alone to be responsible in employment. So one of our most valuable resources has been Manpower's Basic Job Readiness Training Program, which has a 3-month program ideal for many of our clients. Miss

Rhoda Butt has been most helpful in establishing an excellent relationship there, and she in turn has sent us people from the BJRT program to get training working with us as volunteers. But we do also work with other agencies on direct job referrals, and have acquired some resources of our own. Nonetheless, the unemployment problem remains an acute one, and key to the low self-image of many clients. I have often felt that if our government was less satisfied with the high unemployment rate current in Canada, we would lose half of our business.

Alcoholism is another major problem, and we have some excellent counsellors on staff who actively use AA and other programs. AA was probably the first resource we used extensively, and we still find it one of the most wonderful. Another staff member, Ruby Welbourn, has been developing resources in the community for our borderline mentally-ill clients. Many of these can be released to Bail Supervision rather than languishing in jail, if we have suitable supports, which Ms. Welbourn is developing with group homes for community release of the mentally ill.

I could continue, but these examples are sufficient to indicate how important this area is to us, and how far we feel we have come in developing it. Our whole approach has been dynamic rather than static: if we cannot help a client, find a resource that can; if no such resource exists, go out and start one that does.

Conclusion: Summary of Achievements in Program to Date

We have traced the origins and history of the Toronto-York Bail Program, and then discussed how we have responded to each of seven areas common to most new Bail Programs. We now turn to the question of where we are now, what our particular achievements are, and what the future may hold.

Recently, the Director of another program asked me: "Is your program based on the surveillance model or the therapy model of supervision?" I thought a minute and said "How about a third model: that of being a true friend to the client in the community, a friend with knowledge of resources, who can help the clients relate to the resources to meet the goals they have for their own lives?"

I think this conversation epitomizes for me one of our main achievements. Unlike most therapeutic approaches, and unlike most approaches in the Criminal Justice System, we don't think of ourselves as superior beings to our clients. Most of them get into trouble because of a surfeit of creative energy and a lack of appropriate resources for channeling it constructively in our society.

We have authority, and of course, we have to exercise that authority when needed. But most of our clients welcome the opportunity to find some of the new vistas life holds. Alcohol, drugs and property destruction are their escapes, and prisons and courts are society's escape from the shared problem that these people have not found in our society sufficient constructive outlet for the creative potential every person has. We have had some remarkable success stories of dramatic changes in some lives. But more important is that day by day, our clients have come to feel our office is a friendly place where they can be respected now, as they are.

In numerical terms, we are now completing 400–500 verifications a month, and have about 375 persons on supervision, most of whom would be in jail without the program. Our monthly failure rates on "Failures to Appear," "Failures to Comply," and persons arrested with new charges are under 10%. In October to December 1980, we averaged 7% Failure to Appears and 2% of Failure to Comply, and 8% new charges. Although we would always like these still lower, they seem to satisfy the judges, police and crowns when presented to them, and we have no basis of comparsion, since statistics on such rates for those on other forms of release are unavailable.

We have grown past the infancy stage, and our relations with all court parties are in general balanced and positive. We can differ and criticize one another and continue to work together with generally good cooperation. Our staff in general have worked very hard on the business of good relations with those less warm toward the idea of the program, and we have come a long way.

One of our goals has been to retain some of our objectives about the justice system while working within it. Most of our staff are committed to calling for changes when we see they are needed in the system as a whole, as well as "helping individuals." Perhaps that is one of the most important contributions. Overall, we have added one more humanizing agency to the justice system, and one more which takes away a little of the economic discrimination. But the most visible impact to our programs is to see people walk into our office with pride in their step, making new plans with us for a fresh start, who were in jail yesterday, and who would still be there without the program.

NOTES

1. Reprinted from *International Journal of Offender Therapy and Comparative Criminology.* Vol 25, No.2, 1981.

2. Court appointed lawyers who serve all accused in bail court, who are unrepresented at that point, which means nearly all accused, since they have just been arrested.

3. Regina vs. Chicanski, Ontario High Court of Justice, Cromarty, January 1976; and Regina vs. Garrington, et al. Ontario High Court of Justice, O'Driscoll, April 1972.

13.
GROUP HOMES AND THE STRUGGLE FOR
COMMUNITY INTEGRATION

In the course of my personal work with prisoners and exprisoners, I contacted a number of halfway houses to take in my friends, took a number into our own home, and played a key role in the founding of two halfway houses myself, Galbraith Bail Residence and My Brother's Place. In all this I became very aware of the community itself as a major part of the problem, shutting out its own rejected members while blaming them for not achieving integration in spite of the community.

The two papers that follow were written at two different stages of my experience, and for two very different audiences. The first, in 1980, was presented to the North York City Council as a brief on a day when they were considering legislation to widen acceptance of group homes in North York.

The second, more academic paper, was presented to the Second International Conference on Prison Abolition at a workshop there in Amsterdam. This second paper shows the impact of 5 years of experience, the founding of my two halfway houses, and the inroads of the system on several of the alternatives I had worked so hard to establish. It raises many points I will refer to again in the closing part of this section, on the nature of true alternatives to prisons.

BRIEF FOR NORTH YORK ON HOUSING FOR
DISADVANTAGED GROUPS
September 15, 1980

My name is Ruth Morris, and I am a housewife and professional social worker. My husband and I have four children, and own a home in North York; he teaches at York University. For some years we have taken into our home exprisoners. Our friends have not created a crime wave, and have not committed offenses against our neighbors. About the only direct impact on the neighbors was that one of our housebreakers once assisted a neighbor who had locked herself out to get into her own home, making very sure it really was her own home.

One of the most important myths to conquer in discussing this issue is the idea "criminals" are somehow a different kind of creature from the rest of us. The people who come before the courts and fill the jails and prisons are younger and poorer and a little more longhaired than we are, but otherwise, they don't differ a lot from our own adolescent children. One of the first questions wide-eyed volunteers, leaving one of our jail volunteer programs for the first time, usually ask is, "But where are the real criminals?" The population of our jails just doesn't fit the stereotyped image of the TV punk villain.

A number of studies has shown that at least 90% of us have committed some crime serious enough to have served time, had we been caught and prosecuted. "Criminals," as labelled by our justice system, are for the most part those who are enough poorer, more friendless and unskilled to get caught and labelled. When a middle class youngster gets caught, the system notices a few differences, and he usually gets routed so that he doesn't get labelled. All this is relevant because in addressing the question of housing, we have to know who we are talking about, and why we are afraid of them.

I run the Toronto/York Bail Program, so I see through the various courts we serve all those who come before the courts with criminal charges. A great part of our caseload on bail supervision consists of 16 to 18 year olds, almost all from broken homes, many who have been wards of Children's Aid, and in institutions or a succession of foster homes. A lot of them are unemployed youth from other parts of Canada who have come to Toronto in hope of employment, and have limited success.

When I compare their lives with those of my children, I am appalled at the difficulties they have already endured, and amazed at the amount of strength many of them have. In spite of everything most of them still want to make it the right way in our world, but they need a few breaks if they are going to fulfill that dream.

The recent study on the problems of suburbia indicates that as the middle classes have moved in on the inner city, the poor have been squeezed out to the suburbs, where there is inadequate low-priced housing for them, and a lack of appropriate services. We in the suburbs are going to have to be more realistic, or Toronto, of which I am tremendously proud, will deteriorate as American cities have done.

The poor and disadvantaged youth who make up the "criminal population" are going to exist somewhere, until we are ready to attack basic issues of poverty and inequality more effectively than seems likely now. So the only question is, under what conditions will they be living in North York?

Would you rather have a confused 18-year-old with no roots and few job skills living in a room with no guidance, or in a halfway house where he has some supervision and the assistance of social workers who can help him find the support he needs? That is the only issue you can realistically decide.

Thinking about this brief, I remember the first visit I made to a CRC (Community Resource Centres), in which selected people serving sentences spend their last months while working and making money to support their families. Rick, the young man I visited, is one of 10 children from a multi-problem family, with a severely alcoholic father.

Rick was finishing his second prison term, and his joy in being in the CRC, living in a real house with real people around him was like a small child at Christmas. I remember his going outside to rake leaves, and speaking proudly of how he delighted in chatting to the neighbors and having them talk back to him "like I was a regular person." Rick is now working, supporting two children, and making it in the community. The transition period in the CRC was a key factor in his success. Are we too small in North York to give the Ricks of our world a chance to feel like "regular people?"

GROUP HOMES, FAMILIES, AND NEIGHBORHOODS AS STRATEGIC BUILDING BLOCKS TOWARD ABOLITION

INTRODUCTION

For a number of years I have been engaged in promoting alternatives to prisons. Increasingly, I have learned to distinguish between "true" alternatives and so-called alternatives which are merely creating "prisons in the community." In this paper I would like to discuss the following points, concerning group homes as true alternatives building toward the prisonless society:

1) Definition of True Alternatives to Prison

2) Under What Conditions Are Group Homes True Alternatives?

3) My Personal Experience Working for Group Homes

4) Research on Group Homes vs. Community Belief: Pluralistic Ignorance With A Vengeance.

5) A Theory to Explain This Discrepancy, Pointing Toward Solutions

6) Summary & Conclusions: The Place of Group Homes in Building Prison Abolition.

1) DEFINITION OF TRUE ALTERNATIVES TO PRISON

Personally I have spent several years of my life building a variety of so-called alternatives to prison, and building networking groups aimed at transforming the system. In a few short years, I have seen most of these organizations coopted by the system, taken over and dominated as times have moved to the right by people who use them to fill exactly the functions prisons fill. I have seen other so-called "alternatives" that never were alternatives, for from their inception they were designed to widen the net, to stigmatize, to perpetrate vengeance, and to separate "us" from "them."

Thinking about this dilemma a few years ago, as I was fighting to keep the major pretrial alternative I was administering from being swept into this negative syndrome, I came up with some ideas for what distinguishes an alternative from a prison. One of the myths system people try to tell us is that anything we run to keep people nominally out from lock and key is so much better than having them locked up in a building called a prison, that we should make any compromise to get funding and legal permission to run an alternative. Of course the system people love it when we do this: they save money on "alternatives," and we end up lending our character to their methods, incidentally using up our energies for a pittance of their salaries.

For my part, I quickly concluded that my objection to prisons is to something much more oppressive than closed buildings, or even locks and keys. It's important to think this out, because otherwise we delude ourselves about building alternatives when actually we are creating their very spirit in the community, destroying people just as effectively as any building with locks can possibly do. And our actions may be even more destructive, because it is always more upsetting when seemingly "good" people treat you in a demeaning, destructive way than when obviously vicious ones do.

So I hope every one of us has thought about this basic question, and come up with our own answers. There are a lot of ways of expressing it, but I am just going to sum up the main characteristics I am conscious of in prisons which make them destructive, and which we have to avoid in alternatives if they are not going to be just as destructive. Prisons and prison-like institutions promote:

A) Widening the net to regulate lives that would be free without our "alternative."

B) Separation of people from one another: social isolation from the wider society.

C) Categorization of people within the institution into a rigid caste system, with strong separation into the strong-good-staff vs. the bad-weak-disempowered inmate/clients.

D) Longterm stigmatization of people, with inferior clothes, environment, forms of address, privileges and rights, and restrictions reaching far into the future.

E) Promotion of violence as the basic tool of human interaction. Without coercion there would not be inmates, so that the inmate subculture in reaction is violent, setting up its own pecking order of further violence.

Note the progressive degrees of separation along the path of destruction of these characteristics. As a hunting animal cuts a vulnerable deer off from its pack, chases it far from its fellows, worries it to exhaustion and finally destroys it, the injustice system first catches its prey in its widened net, then separates it, categorizes it rigidly, stigmatizes it still further, and finally exposes it to destructive violence. "Alternatives" which cooperate with this process of hounding their clients to destruction are entirely prisonlike in their processes, however much they may achieve in the way of public recognition, funding, and staff careers.

It does not take much imagination to see from the above list that many social institutions, including many so-called alternatives to prison, have a large measure of these characteristics. In contrast to these dehumanizing and destructive directions, a true alternative to prison must rise above these qualities by such practices as:

Treating clients and staff both in an egalitarian, humane way, showing respect for their value as human beings with rights to justice and dignity.

Integrating all its participants into the total community as positively as possible, on as many fronts as possible.

Rejecting labelling, stigmatizing, and authoritarian controls as far as practicable.

Demonstrating nonviolent ways of resolving problems, by assisting clients in resolving problems such as illegal police violence through advocating for and with them by all legal, educational, and political means available.

Refusing to buy a place in the justice system by a policy of silence toward the demeaning of clients in order to win favour with other institutions which are demeaning clients.

It can readily be seen that few present day alternatives approach these standards. We compromise both individually and as groups in order to continue to have access, because we are convinced that we will still be more humane than those other less caring people who would be there if we weren't. This is the nature of cooptation, and of course, no one can work with the system without being subjected to it. How we resolve it is to some degree an individual matter. But I am suggesting these general measures as guidelines so that we know how far we have gone toward building a prison in the community.

2) UNDER WHAT CONDITIONS ARE GROUP HOMES TRUE ALTERNATIVES?

Probably everyone here is aware that some group homes are more prisonlike than some prisons. I remember reading the rules of one comparatively good group home for ex-cons which had counts several times in every 24 hours. The counts were phoned in to the local prison, which supervised security for them. Anyone in more than 5 minutes after the curfew had to be reported to that prison and returned forthwith. I remember a prison chaplain who argued that it was right that a man was sent back from another group home because out of compassion the resident failed to wake up his keeper-counsellor who was asleep on the job, when the resident returned from a pass on time - as a result of which the resident was mistakenly reported AWOL. I have also heard a number of stories of men who were sent back basically for the sin of not being able to find a job in this economy: the rules of the group home were that you were working, and if you didn't find a job after X amount of weeks, too bad.

Without proliferating horror stories, I think we can agree that some group homes are prisons in the community. But some come wonderfully close to being true alternatives. One in Toronto run for years by an ex-con continually holds the line against parole. It observes good rules for the house and the men, and refuses to make their home a prison run by parole regulations and regimentation.

Even beyond the issue of how group homes for those caught in the criminal justice net straddle the line between system regulations and freedom, there are some more fundamental questions about group homes as alternatives. The very existence of group homes for a particular population labels them as a handicapped group, disadvantaged by society. Who ever heard of group homes for executives, or athletic champs, or gifted children? One can look at group homes as a safety net preserving those who have fallen through the crevices in our family and community resources from plummeting into the abyss of institutions. But isn't a safety net still a net? Aren't group homes by definition less an expression of the caring community than individualized foster home care would be?

Personally, I think they are, and I think those of us who are abolitionists need to work more on supporting individual families and groups who want to take in exprisoners by ones and twos. But meanwhile, group homes which are small, personal, and run in the right spirit can be one positive expression, filling the gap effectively. To fill that gap, however, I think group homes have to fulfill a number of conditions. They have to be:

A) Small: Too many group homes are mini-institutions, their very size mirroring institutional life, and depersonalizing those caught in them. Financial incentives encourage maximizing number of beds to break even, because government funders offer low per diem rates.

B) Determined to place the welfare of the individuals they serve above the steady chipping away of compromises with the system, while still maintaining sufficient rapport with the system to be allowed to run.

C) Integrated into the community. Group homes have to bridge the gaps created by our social system. Even while they accept a special group stigmatized by our current social values, they have to find ways to heal the gap created by those values. Healing the men and women inside the home is not sometimes half so hard as healing the neighbors around from their greater handicap of self-righteousness and bigotry.

D) Willing to be a longterm family for some of their people. Group homes that turn out those who have found acceptance for the first time in their lives after a few weeks or months, and expect them to be totally "independent" are like the families which originally rejected these men and women. A home is a home, and although it does not breed eternal total dependence, neither does it cut off its grown children from contact, or eject them before they are ready for independence.

3)   MY PERSONAL EXPERIENCE WITH GROUP HOMES

Personally I have been intimately involved with group homes for some years. Although I have never staffed one, I was founding Board Chairperson 5 years ago for the first Bail Residence in North America. Currently I am Board Chair for My Brothers' Place, a group home designed to serve 8 chronically institutionalized men who have spent most of their lives between prisons and mental hospitals – a group usually rejected by most group homes as too hard to serve, too sure to fail. I have also testified and written letters for more progressive neighborhood policies on this issue, and organized a local group of neighbors to support group homes coming to our neighborhood when all hell broke loose over the advent of 4 group homes for severely retarded and physically handicapped adults. What the threat was supposed to be I still cannot fathom, as these people were so disabled they could not even walk. But we had 1000 people screaming at a rally that reminded some of the Hitler rallies, and signs all over the neighborhood saying, "No Group Homes in North York." I'm happy to say that those group homes have been operating with total acceptance for about a year, and that our support group was mildly helpful in stemming the tide of hysteria.

I also experimented briefly with forming a linkage of neighborhood groups which had supported group homes in the neighborhoods, and have worked closely with the Supportive Housing Coalition, a networking group assisting groups trying to start new group homes for ex-mental patients. David White, their staffperson and a former Alderman in Toronto, is probably the most knowledgable person in Toronto on facilitating entry of group homes to new neighborhoods, and he has been enormously helpful to homes beyond his own network. David says he is beginning to feel he could write a standard script for these events.

Although the method pioneered by Supportive Housing Coalition and based on Metro Toronto's suggested standards has been quite successful in integrating homes for ex-mental patients with relatively little fuss, it has been somewhat less successful for exprisoners. We have had two really major uproars in the past few years, one of which succeeded in getting rid of the group home. It was this "success," because of the withdrawal of funds by Federal Corrections for the house, which of course stimulated more such efforts.

145

The method used by Supportive Housing Coalition and endorsed by Metro Toronto is to develop excellent outreach materials, to train your Board and Staff and Volunteers with in-depth role playing and planning, and the moment you close the deal for your house, to go to 200-400 neighbors knocking on doors to tell them of your coming to the neighborhood. Although these door to door encounters are similar to political work, they also raise questions for me:

Doesn't the very act of knocking on the door in effect to warn the neighbors suggest a problem?

Is this really the best educational tool or way to change negative attitudes, or to prevent negative attitues from developing?

How many of us would feel comfortable at knocking on a few hundred prospective neighbors' doors before we move into a home, and asking them if they would like us as neighbors, by naming our most unsaleable quality? For example, "I just want to let you know I'm moving into your neighborhood in 2 months, and looking foward to being your neighbor. I had a regular problem with bedwetting till I was adolescent, but I'm quite OK now, and sure you will welcome me..."

I am not faulting Supportive Housing Coalition for doing a wonderful job in an almost impossible situation. I am faulting our Provincial Government for wanting to save money on group homes, but being unwilling to do a major political educational job on it. Consequently they have left groups and individuals in the community to bear the fire of a controversy that could be greatly moderated if not eliminated by an intensive public educational campaign.

This raises the further question of how much of the energies of prison abolitionists should be devoted to promoting and running group homes, a mode sanctioned by governments to save money, instead of saving our energies for direct advocacy and political activities. Yet to achieve abolition I believe we also have to have demonstration models of true alternatives, and the right kinds of group homes are such an alternative. If abolitionists don't pioneer in new areas, as I have, the group homes may well all be prisons in the community, a cheaper, closer substitute for the larger more concrete variety.

If we do go to the trouble of starting a group home, we have to be willing to stick with it. Those who want a prison in the community will take it over if you leave it, for they are less creative than abolitionists, and are generally waiting in the wings to take it over and make a living off of fitting into the system with it if you let go. The price of liberty for the victims of the system is eternal vigilance – for abolitionists.

4) RESEARCH ON GROUP HOMES vs. COMMUNITY BELIEF: PLURALISTIC IGNORANCE WITH A VENGEANCE

Goffman suggests that incongruities in life are the best seed for creative sociological insights. There is a glaring incongruity in this area. Simply put:

> An impressive body of research literature has documented in a variety of places and under varying conditions that group homes do not cause property values to drop, nor do they add disruptive elements to neighborhoods. A recent Toronto study, for instance, showed that group homes for exprisoners caused no drop in property values and no increase in crime or other measurable social problems.[1] Another study showed that within a few years of their founding, group homes are not even known to exist by a majority of their near neighbors, so slight is their actual impact.

> In contrast to this reality, most cities I have visited in North America in the past 2–3 years report controversies over group homes parallel to the panic over neighborhood integration of blacks in an earlier decade. There is massive fear of them, and resistance in many cities and neighborhoods.

How can one account for this incongruity? All behaviour is caused, however irrational or irritating it may be to us. So let us think about possible causes for this glaring discrepancy between documented research and popular belief about group homes.

5) A THEORY TO EXPLAIN THE DISCREPANCY BETWEEN RESEARCH AND POPULAR BELIEF ABOUT GROUP HOMES

One of the most relevant variables in reactions to group homes is that the very areas which are most overburdened already with social problems tend to be most tolerant of group homes. Suburban upper middle class areas which are full of educated people who have had a chance to study social problems, and who have plenty of resources to assist those in group homes are most militantly opposed to any group homes in their midst. They use their political sophistication to pull every string they have to make it politically impossible for group homes to access their areas.

Thus resistance to group homes is clearly not a reflection of a lack of energy or resources to assimilate needy people. On the contrary, resistance seems highest where the group home population seems most different. The more homogenously elite are the residents of an area, the more resistance they are likely to show to the location of group homes, generally comprised of the most powerless in our society. So it would appear that resistance to group homes is part of a pattern of pressure toward homogeneity in society in general, and in modern urban enclaves in particular. Urban dwellers have to learn to live with a marked degree of class and cultural difference within our large cities, in contrast to the comparative homogeneity of small towns. One of their coping devices has been the formation of relatively uniform enclaves within the large multicultural, multiracial, multiclass urban environment:

.   Racial Ghettoes

.   Tightly Uniform Ethnic Clusterings

.   Class Segregation by Similar Priced Housing within Neighborhoods

Resistance to group homes, like resistance to racial integration, may be only one manifestation to clinging to the enclave form of adjustment to urban diversity. But the pressure toward homogeneity in cities conflicts with our value in building the caring community through acceptance of diversity. Neighborhood resistance to group homes may be not bigotry, but a desperate clinging to one remaining straw of control to maintain neighborhood homogeneity in our bewilderingly diverse urban society. Nevertheless, it conflicts with our goal of integrating victims of the criminal injustice system into the mainstream of society. If the conflict we encounter in this field is the stress bewteen the integration needed for the caring community and the homogeneity desperately sought by the anomic urban dweller, where can we look for solutions?

6) SUMMARY AND CONCLUSIONS: GROUP HOMES AND PRISON ABOLITION

Perhaps the answer lies in extending our compassion to the anomic urban dweller, and using our group homes creatively to build bridges of understanding where we now have chasms of fear. We need to respect and understand the fear of difference, while finding ways to bridge it. So the prison abolitionist working to build group homes needs to work on three fronts at once;

Showing absolute respect for the group home's residents, making sure our treatment of them is totally different in character from that of a prison.

Challenging the system where it needs challenging, while continuing to work with it in order to run the group home.

Understanding the fears and pressures toward homogeneity of the neighborhood, while finding ways to transcend those fears by building bridges of understanding.

If we can be true to our principles on all these three fronts, we can build group homes which will have a significant part in prison abolition. Group homes can be the basis for a real first home for friendless victims of the socio-economic and justice system. They can be a cutting edge, calling the injustice system to justice. Finally, they can help our fearful neighborhoods, instead of building fences of fear, to find security in newly created trust, and through understanding diversity to share with us in building the caring community.

C. Lowe & S. Hussein, "Community Impact Study: The Effect of Locating Correctional Group Homes in Residential Neighborhoods." Canadian Training Instute, direction of John Sawdon, Kinsman Building, York University, 4700 Keele St., Downview, Ontario, Canada, 1984.

4.
THE MAGIC OF MEDIATION: A FIRST-LINE ALTERNATIVE

In 1985 I had the opportunity to found a community mediation service (St. Stephen's Conflict Resolution Service) in the Kensington area of Toronto, on of the most multicultural neighborhoods in Canada. The discussion which follows owes much to pioneers in the field of community mediation: Dave Worth, Mark Yantzi, Ray Shonholz, and Ken Hawkins.

Community mediation services have been touted for some years as an ideal first-line alternative to prisons and courts, because they reach into the very heart of the community itself. Free of the punitive, labelling taint of the court system, community mediation services appear to offer a fresh breath of clean air to the alternatives field. In fact, they do offer a very hopeful model, but they too are too often caught between the devil and the deep blue sea in the struggle to build true alternatives.

Two broad options are open to communtiy mediation programs:

1) Retaining a community-based footing, mediating cases from the community itself, and avoiding direct connections to the court system, either by referrals or funding.

2) Becoming in some sense an adjunct service of the courts, accepting referrals from them for a significant proportion of their cases, accepting the conditions imposed by the courts, and usually having substantial funding from the courts.

There are advantages each way, and Ray Shonholz has pointed out that more and more newer mediation programs are choosing the second option. It solves the two biggest challenges of mediation services: getting adequate ongoing funding, and getting a consistent large flow of cases for mediation. But mediation services tied to the courts often have to swallow many of the punitive, labelling rules of the court, and may lose the very qualities that make them true alternatives to the whole hierarchical system of vengeance.

On the other hand, community-based services have their own problems Not only do few of them solve successfully the twin dilemmas of inadequate funding sources and the difficulty of persuading enough disputants to bring conflicts to them, but they often get caught in dealing almost exclusively with cases which are very unlikely ever to come to court. This leaves the really serious conflicts still to the court system.

In spite of these difficulties, community mediation does offer one of the most positive, genuine alternatives to the whole penal approach to justice. What I propose to explore here are two important points:

The gift of communtiy mediation, and what it offers in really healing community conflict.

Three principal sources of resistance to wider and more effective application of mediation as a true alternative.

THE GIFT OF COMMUNITY MEDIATION

Often in doing mediation training I refeed to the magic of the process. The mediation process we use is patterned after the San Francisco Boards' model, which has the following assumptions.

1) Conflict is normal and universal. In dealing with it constructively, we need to accept our responsibility to seek help in resolving it.

2) An effective conflict resolution needs to be inclusive: including all affected parties in the conflict, and including a spectrum (3-5) of trained volunteers from the community itself, representative of the same kinds of people as the disputants.

3) The tools of empathy, validation, clarification and summarization, effectively used by the mediators, provide the safety and support needed by the vast majority of disputants to be empowered to resolve their own conflict. These tools are reinforced by the twin safety groundrules: don't interrupt, and show respect.

4) All kinds of disputes are amenable to this process. Because conflict is normal and healthy, we should take pride in using this process, and confidentiality should not be a major issue, though it is available for those who want it.

The process itself follows three major steps, but even before these steps an important beginning occurs in the welcome and introduction. The general nature of each step is outlined below, along with the inner experiences that disputants go through in a successful mediation:

CONTENT:	DISPUTANT EXPERIENCES:
Welcome & Introduction Disputants are warmly welcomed by each mediator. Introductions occur which link and give hope. Process and ground rules are explained.	1. I am welcomed and protected here.
Step One Disputants talk to panel, each outlining their feelings and concerns. Panel validates their feelings, summarizes the concerns of each.	2. I am being heard. 3. My opponent is being heard. 4. I am cared about. 5. My opponent is cared about. 6. It is possible for these people to care about us both at the same time! 7. We are rewarded by the mediators when we recognize each other's needs.
Step Two Disputants talk to each other, with the goal that they are able to hear each other as well as the panel has heard both.	8. I can hear my opponent. 9. My opponent can hear me! 10. I can care about my opponent. 11. My opponent is caring about me.
Step Three Disputants are invited to brainstorm solutions together, now that they have shown ability to hear each other's solutions.	12. We can find solutions together!

The magic of this process is such that over 90% of disputants using it are able to find solutions, and these solutions hold up at a 3-month follow-up in 80% of cases (San Francisco Boards figures over 10 year period). But the magic is much more experiential than that. When you see former friends who have been so bitterly opposed they cannot even greet one another or look into each other'eyes, exchange a clandestine hug after such a session, you begin to experience the wonder of this magic yourself. The magic infects mediators: the process is so validating to all concerned that I experience personal growth in every mediation I do. Where does this magic come from?

THE SOURCE OF THE MAGIC

Recently I gained some insight into the source of the magic. All of us have within us defense attorneys and crown prosecutors. Unless we are unusually hostile people, most of the time our defense attorneys are in charge when we meet a new person. If the relationship is to prosper, the defense attorney interprets three sets of data all favorably:

POSITIVE DATA: Nice things the person does, are registered as proof of his virtue and goodness.

NEUTRAL DATA: Things which could be interpreted either way. "She went to the movies that day" is interpreted as, "She is willing to go out and seek active social entertainment." (Positive interpretation of all neutral data.)

NEGATIVE DATA: Things which on the surface seem negative, are interpreted as lovable little faults. "She failed her exams" is interpreted as, "She is so dedicated to our organization that she gave her study time to it, isn't that wonderful!"

When a friendship or working relationship begins to deteriorate, the Crown Attorney gradually comes more and more to the fore. At first attempts are made to patch things up, and he is constantly pushed back. But if patchup efforts by the disputants themselves continue to fail, eventually the Crown Attorney takes over altogether.

Now all data is interpreted in the most negative possible light: the Crown Attorney bends not only present data but reinterprets past data in the light of the new hostile situation. Lovable faults become terrible behaviour; neutral data becomes threatening; and positive data is hypocrisy. History is rewritten in this light: now we understand many things we looked on favorably in the past in a wholly new and wholly negative way. The Crown Attorney makes his case overwhelmingly, for any kind of data fits into it. Even peace overtures are interpreted as a plot.

Unresolved bitter conflicts never come back from this situation: the Crown Attorney has won and the relationship either severs or continues totally bitter. But there are a number of ways of turning even the worst situation around, so that in effect, a kindly judge (alas, missing in courts) takes over. The kindly, wise judge cannot take things back to where the defense attorney had them, for now the Crown's data, some of which is undeniable, has to be considered too. But the judge acknowledges many of the Crown's points, yet reminds the court that much the Defense Attorney had to say is true too, and reinterprets the findings in the light of both. The judge concludes with directions for a new relationship, one which recognizes the validity of some of the painful experiences brought out by the Crown, but which also takes account of the strengths the Defense has pointed out. The judge helps work out a resolution consistent with all the data, but one which rebuilds the relationship in some measure.

I'm aware of three ways I've seen the kindly judge take over and reverse a hostile, deteriorating relationship. One is old-fashioned unilateral forgiveness. Sometimes one party chooses to be big enough to say, "Enough. Regardless of how wronged I feel, this person is valuable, and I am going to live forgiveness whatever he/she does." Such a solo action is rare and hard, nor does it always draw an accepting response. But it is growing for the person daring to try it, and can evoke a very positive response, single-handedly bringing the kindly judge into power in both lives.

More often, even after previous attempts at dialogue have failed, the two disputants together may arrive at an understanding in a last attempt to talk it out, which enables the kindly judge to regain control of the situation in both their lives. But Conflict Resolution is the third way, and the only way in the many situations where neither the two together nor either one alone has been able to reverse the rising power of the Crown Attorney. Conflict Resolution is far the most potent way of giving the kindly judge ascendancy, for the mediators model the judge's benevolent process, which has to take place internally in each disputant, and the mediators set up ideal conditions in which the kindly judge has more scope to operate than the Crown Attorney.

SOURCES OF RESISTANCE TO
USE OF MEDIATION AS A TRUE ALTERNATIVE

I am aware of three important sources of resistance to mediation's wider use as a true alternative to penal justice:

1) Individual resistance to taking responsibility for our conflicts.
2) Institutional/structural resistance to alternatives in general.
3) Mediation's weakness in coping with power inequalities.

1. INDIVIDUAL RESISTANCE

The difficulty most mediation services have in getting cases for mediation is certainly not from a shortage of bitter conflicts in our lives. Conflict is everywhere, causes us incredible hardships, and our methods of dealing with it wreak great personal and social havoc. Why then do mediation services have to struggle desperately to get a token number of cases for mediation?

Being a disputant in mediation is not easy. It requires that we take ownership and responsibility for our part in the dispute. Not only is this hard because we wrongly label disputants as sick or bad, it is also hard because taking responsibility means we cannot use the tactic of the criminal justive system in passing all the guilt and all the responsibility and all the punitive experiences on to someone conveniently labelled "criminal," who just happens to be from a lower social class and power group.

In short, accepting mediation individually as an alternative to things now dealt with in courts requires a revolution in our thinking. We have to accept our own responsibility for our part in the social system which generates the thing we call "crime," and our own responsibility to participate in healing its causes and effects. This requires a great educational effort, and an attitudinal change in our society.

2. STRUCTURAL RESISTANCE

Like all other altenatives, mediation as a major alternative is a threat to all those who make their living and who gain their sense of place from the existing punitive justice system. Lawyers, judges, police, guards and many others including many social service workers are enmeshed in the status quo and consciously or unconsciously fight to defend it. An ironic bit in a demonstration film on our program shows an amazingly successful and creative mediation of a serious theft, and interpolates our Attorney General in Ontario saying that mediation is fine for civil cases, but wholly inappropriate in any criminal matter!

3.   WEAKNESS OF MEDIATION IN DEALING WITH POWER INEQUALITIES

Mediation does not solve power inequalities. First of all, it is extremely hard to get the more powerful party to mediation, where great power inequality exists. Secondly, the whole process and the resolutions are affected by power inequalities. Example: a battering husband and his submissive wife, if they ever get to mediation, may happily agree on a resolution of his only beating her in certain circumstances, less frequent than hitherto practiced!

But if mediation deals poorly with power inequalities, courts and prisons are worse. Class and power bias are overwhelming and nakedly oppressive in them. In most mediation, the mediation agency and the mediators consciously strive to modify power differences as far as they can, and to give some protection and greater voice to weaker parties. Though in the end they have to accept the parties' patterns if one has always dominated the other, they usually do move the line a little nearer toward equality, while the courts widen the gap and solidify oppression in most cases.

It may be argued that courts protect the weak too – superficially this is often so, but usually underneath the superficial protection of a weak citizen is the blind oppression of an even weaker "criminal."

What is clear is that neither mediation nor courts resolve power inequalities. Advocacy, lobbying, social action, and political action are essential tools for dealing with this major problem.

CONCLUSION

Mediation is one of the most exciting tools of the alternative movement. Both socially and individually, its potential is great. But like other alternatives, it is not a free gift. We have to struggle to establish its true position and its appropriate acceptance and use.

To operate as a true alternative, mediation needs to have enough distance from court restrictions to retain its alternative flavour and character. Public education on mediation needs to be widespread enough so that people are much more widely willing to accept their role as disputants, that conflict is normal, and that all of us have to take responsibility for sharing in resolving our conflicts by bringing them to mediation, and working at this very positive process. Systemic resistances have to be overcome, as with all alternatives. And finally, we have to become so committed to mediation as a society that more powerful parties feel as committed to using it as less powerful parties; while we continue to labor at the roots of injustice in power inequality through political and social action beyond mediation itself.

5.
WHAT TO DO WITH THE
VIOLENT/SEXUAL OFFENDERS

This basic question is always among the first one asked of abolitionists:"But what would you do with the really dangerous ones?" It is impossible, therefore, to write a book on abolition without devoting a short section at least, to direct answers. Yet, before I attempt to respond to it, I want to stress again that the myth that the prison system exists primarily for dangerous offenders is

157

just that, a myth. Gilbert Cantor, a former editor of *The Shingle,* the magazine of the Philadelphia Bar Association, has written an outstanding article called "An End To Crime And Punishment," from which we will quote a good deal. The amazing thing is that this brilliant exposition on ending the entire criminal justice system, written by an eminent member of the Bar in May, 1976, and featured as their entire issue by *The Shingle,* burst on the scene so long ago, and its truths are still largely unheard. Cantor has some specific ideas about dealing with the dangerous few, to which we will allude later, but here we merely want to underline his point about perspective:"In no event can we allow our fear of these few persons to dictate a penal system which controls more than 1,300,000 persons at any given time."[1]

Yet that is precisely what we do. The entire court and prison system is always defended on the ground that they are necessary for containment of the dangerous few. Cantor goes on to explain the fallacy of this:"We have among us at all times a large number of people who will sooner or later commit violent acts. Most of these people are undetected and, in practical and also constitutional terms, undetectable as to their violent potential. The release under restrictive conditions of certain previously violent persons, though somewhat hazardous in particular cases, will not actually increase the dangerousness of the world in which we live. In the case of the vast majority of offenders, our refusal to imprison will diminish the likelihood of future violence so that the net result of the entire decriminalization program will be a safer or less violent society."[2]

Three important points emerge from this. First, the prison system is NOT dealing primarily with the dangerous few, but rather with the hapless multitude. Second, far from protecting us, it makes the dangerous few more dangerous. Finally, prison itself is a violence creating environment that makes some previously nondangerous people become dangerous.

Another difficulty in tackling this subject is the difficulty of identifying who are the truly dangerous ones. Although most Canadians would agree on Clifford Olson as one, and perhaps a handful of specific others, beyond that, disagreements arise, and there is no solid evidence that psychiatrists, judges, or any other "experts" can successfully identify who is and is not a future dangerous offender, even when previous violent behaviour exists. The frightening bias against people of the wrong social class, skin color, or with unsavoury manners, leads these groups to be overclassified as dangerous, compared to smoother, more middle class types. Honey Knopf and her Prison Education Action Project have done a lot of excellent research on programs for chronic sex offenders and the violent few. They advocate "restraint where necessary while re-education and re-training occur." They further state that no one should ever be excluded from humane conditions, or the opportunity for changing violent, physically harmful behaviour.

One more important point to remember about the violent offender is that there is overwhelming evidence that in most cases violent offenders are acting out their part in a cycle of violence. Abused as children, they pass it on in terrifying violence at the world, as adults. Perpetuating the violence cycle by a violent response ourselves does not break the cycle, it merely identifies one player in a chain of violence as the "bad one," and justifies more violence toward him/her.

Parker Rossman, in a searching book called *After Punishment, What,* about juvenile offenders with serious violent offences, describes success by one judge who recommends three steps: intensive supervision, confrontation with victims, and restitution.[3]

Cantor, after describing use of the civil courts for money damages, while enhancing the financial means of indigent offenders, recommends extension of the system to dangerous offenders. "My proposal, as outlined in this chaper, would apply even to the 'savage few' who apparently cannot be 'civilized'-- those who are not treated within the mental health system, but who appear to lack the will or the power to avoid violent behaviour. The program designed for such a person -- subject always to imprisonment for contempt -- must provide sufficient restriction and supervision to result in apprehension for any occasion or threat of violence."[4]

Basically then, the answers that seem to be available now fall into the following categories:

1) SEPARATION:
Some kind of temporary, humane separation for the mutual protection of the individual and society may be necessary at some point, most abolitionists agree, but recognize that separation itself, unless carefully handled, may aggravate the problem.

2)   RE-EDUCATION OR TREATMENT:

Both of. these concepts can be offensive, and as dangerous if misused as imprisonment, yet in the face of extremely violent behaviour, some effort to reorient the person's behaviour seems essential. P.R.E.A.P. suggests that self-help groups with outside guidance are most effective in helping incest violators to come to awareness that their behaviour is unacceptable.

3)   INTENSIVE SUPERVISION:

Both Rossman and Cantor suggest some form of intensive supervision of violent or potentially violent persons in the community may be a major answer. The cost of employing an enthusiastic person or persons with counselling training full time in working with one person in the community is less than many options currently used, aside from the greater ethical and social merits of it. Recently in Winnipeg I saw the full time employment of two young men to live with and help adapt a severely retarded and chronically institutionalized man whom institutions had also made emotionally disturbed. If we are willing to invest so much in resources for him, why not use this as a model for others?

4)   RESPONSE TO VICTIMS:

In some way, the violent offender needs to be made aware of the meaning of his actions for others, and helped to be part of the healing in the lives he/she has damaged. A tall order, but a necessary one. Without such awareness, the violent person goes on responding to the internalized violence inside him/herself from childhood without perceiving the real lives around now being damaged by violence.

A further difficulty in answering this question lies in our unreality about violence and its prevalence in our society. Research and feminist advocacy widen almost daily our awareness of how widespread are incest, rape, and battering of women. If indeed these practices are very widespread,then the violent, dangerous offender is merely the tip of the iceberg, and real social remedies lie in redefining our values, rooting out sexual oppression and power oppression in our socialization process. We also need to modify the winner-take-all and anything-goes-to-win values.

In short, we have no final answers to the violent few. The final answers lie in the wisdom of a society which is willing to devote more effort to looking at this real problem, and less in the fallacy of prisons, using them to add to social oppression for the multitude of nonviolent offenders. We have to look at the roots of violence in our social values. Meanwhile, we need to devote more attention to serious research on the best ways of treating them through temporary separation, re-education, supervision, and relating them to the meaning of their acts through contact with victims. And we have to recognize once and for all that prisons do not solve violence: they create it.

6.
THE SPIRIT OF TRUE ALTERNATIVES

In my paper on Group Homes, I outlined many of my thoughts on true alternatives. A true alternative models, in the way its staff and board treat clients and one another, the kind of behaviour we want the clients to adopt. A true alternative always acts on issues which come to the alternative agency directly as part of their work, and directly affects their clients and staff. A true alternative never goes on doing a tightly defined job precisely, while people are dying in the cracks all around and between the agencies.

True alternatives have five major characteristics:

1) Respect
2) Integrating People
3) Democratic Processes
4) Advocacy
5) Honesty

RESPECT:
True alternatives treat clients and staff with respect for their value as human beings.

INTEGRATING PEOPLE:
True alternatives work at integrating clients and staff into the total community as broadly as possible, but they never accept integration of some part (the administration, for example, to gain agency "credibility") at the price of honesty, or fair play for others.

DEMOCRATIC PROCESSES:
True alternatives reject labelling, stigmatizing, and authoritarian controls as far as possible.

ADVOCACY:
True alternatives demonstrate nonviolent problem solving by assisting clients to advocate for their rights on such issues as illegal police violence and other oppression.

HONESTY:
True alternatives refuse to buy a place in the justice system by a policy of silence about the demeaning of clients.

These principles need to be applied to each type of alternative, and the struggle to live them out is a daily one. The day to day decisions of every alternative agency on these issues determine how far we as a society are providing true alternatives to prisons.

Until we build and maintain a network of true alternatives to prisons for the varied needs we have, prisons will be merely a more honest manifestation of a spirit of hierarchy and oppression which colours too many of their so-called alternatives. Yet I do not regret the years I have spent building alternatives. We must continue the struggle to achieve the spirit they represent, and we must accept our failures as challenges to learn from, besting our opponents not in vindictive in-fighting, which is their forte, but in a spirit which never ceases to work for a world where mutual respect for human rights dominates all our social institutions.

PART IV
CONCLUSIONS:
PRISON ABOLITION TODAY AND TOMORROW

Prison abolition has a long and honorable history. Writers such as Victor Hugo and Charles Dickens pointed out movingly the class oppression, destructiveness, and injustice of the prison and justice system of their day. My first professor of criminology, Negley Teeters, startled me both in his classic text and in his class in 1956, by the statement: "If we opened all the prison doors today, it would make no impact on the amount of crime."

Two questions need to be answered:

1) Given all the reasons for prison abolition, why is the movement only beginning to gain significance, and even losing many battles?

2) Given all the systemic resistances to abolition, what are the strengths of the movement which give it viability, even in right-wing times, and hope for the future?

SYSTEMIC RESISTANCE TO ABOLITION

Obviously a major source of resistance is the large institutional appraratus that depends on the existing system for jobs and power. This is easy to see, but a more universal source of resistance is the psychological satistaction we get from projecting all the evil in our own hearts and in the world onto scapegoats who can be punished on behalf of it all. As Reiwald observes, "Society appears to fight the criminal with all its strength, but in practice, it does everything to retain him."

Closely related to this factor, but somewhat beyond it, the prison system reinforces class and power barriers.

Fourthly, it offers pseudo-security in a world where there can be no real security against accident, disease, and human hurt. Especially in the absence of widespread religious security through living faith, we cling desperately to the vestige of security prisons and courts offer us, in the face of violence and evil, not realizing that in creating and supporting prisons, we ourselves add significantly to evil in the world.

STRENGTHS OF THE ABOLITION MOVEMENT

The basic strength of prison abolition lies in the fundamental truths on which it is based. In the long run, truth always will prevail.

In 1984, I wrote an editorial in our Abolition Newsmagazine, in which I described the path by which the prison system itself is constantly making new abolitionists for us:

THE ROAD TO ABOLITION

This issue is on strategies toward abolition: the attrition model; direct political action such as demonstrations and protests; and changes aimed at the root cause of all economic and political oppression in our society.

All these methods are different ways of breaking into the chicken and egg cycle, to work toward basic change. We abolitionists have to choose not so much among different methods, as how to move people along the road toward abolition. Once we get enough people there, we'll create abolition because we *won't be able to live with prisons.*

The path to social awareness on prisons is like a pilgrimage:

GANGBUSTERS:
Some people never turn into it, and go through life thinking gangbusters is the whole story on crime and punishment, prisons and courts.

GLIMPSERS:
Others have some brief exposure: a course that touches on the miseries and injustice, a friend who gets into trouble, a visit to a court. They have a vague uneasy awareness that it is not all as simple as the FBI or RCMP make out, but they never go any further with it.

REHABILITATORS:
Those who go one step further get involved with some individuals caught in the system, and care about them. People at this stage of involvement are still trying to "rehabilitate criminals," to save the souls of those who have gone astray, but they may be very compassionate in their

outreach. If sensitive, they are increasingly aware that society too is partly responsible for the situation.

REFORMERS:
If they are still open, at some point they will reach the next marker along the way, and become at least as concerned with what society is doing to prisoners, and has done to make them prisoners, as the other way round. People who get this far are social activists, but they are still prison reformers.

ABOLITIONISTS:
The final turn toward abolition comes when you become aware that prisons can't be reformed because the causes of their injustice and destructiveness are in the very nature of our prison and court systems. Abolitionists also recognize that the twin prison spirits of Revenge and Inequality reach their tentacles into many areas of our social and economic system. In the end we see that to abolish prisons we must give up the privileges that our passive acceptance of police, court, and prison violence bring us.

Meanwhile, those of us who have come thus far on the journey need to work patiently and understandingly with those at all points along the way. Nurturing growth in social awareness is Abolition in Action.

Yet the system also wears down, coopts, or throws out many of the abolitionists it helps to create. Attrition is a two-way process: abolitionists beat upon the system, and the system beats upon us. I described this process in a conference review on our Conference of "What to do With Violent Sexual Offenders," in 1984:

"Personally, having viewed over 10 years the casualties among delicated people starting out with these goals, I could write feelingly how one by one we are absorbed (coopted), our energies transferred into endless healing of the increasing individual suffering or ejected, in this attrition approach.

"If we do not keep fresh waves coming, our brief beating upon the unfeeling stone of the injustice system will be like the solitary wave which crashes once upon the rock and is lost. But if through conferences like this and continued faithfulness with whatever we have left to give, we can keep fresh waves coming to beat upon the intransigent rock, then gradually the water, for all its seeming softness, wears away even the rock.

"For this reason I rejoice when I see at such conferences new faces setting out on the same hard road of growth I have travelled, and I hope they will share the joys and sorrows, and in their pulsing growth, wash just a little more of that solid rock away."

This dual rock of attrition, this beating of truth upon stone and stone upon truth, is the abolition process. Claire Culhane rightly calls it "the best fight in town."

A reporter in 1983, after listening to me for some time, asked mildly, "Don't you think all this stuff is spitting into the wind?"

Without hestitation I responded spontaneously, "No, I believe we are the wind of the future." This book is written for all those who have chosen to be part of that wind of the future.

NOTES

1. Gilbert Cantor, "An End To Crime And Punishment: *The Shingle*, May. 1976, Vol. 39, No.6. Philadelphia, Penn., pp. 111–112.

2. Ibid., p.112

3. Parker Rossman, *After Punishment, What.* William Collins, Cleveland, 1980, p. 114.

4. Cantor, "An End To Crime And Punishment," *The Shingle*, May 1976. Philadelphia Bar Association, Philadelphia, Vol. 39, No. 6, p.111.

BIBLIOGRAPHY

Instead of Prisons. Prison Research Education Action Project. Syracuse, 1976.

In Place of Prisons. Dennis Briggs. Toward a New Society, 1975.

6 Quakers Look At Crime And Punishment. Quaker Home Service, London, 1979.

3518

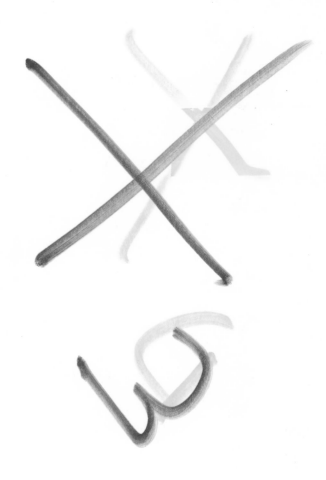